FORWARD/COMMENTARY

The National Institute of Standards and Technology (NIST) is a measurement standards laboratory, and a non-regulatory agency of the **United States Department of Commerce**. Its mission is to promote innovation and industrial competitiveness. Founded in 1901, as the National Bureau of Standards, NIST was formed with the mandate to provide standard weights and measures, and to serve as the national physical laboratory for the United States. **With a** world-class measurement and testing laboratory encompassing a wide range of areas of computer science, mathematics, statistics, and systems engineering, NIST's cybersecurity program supports its overall mission to promote U.S. innovation and industrial competitiveness by advancing measurement science, standards, and related technology through research and development in ways that enhance economic security and improve our quality of life.

The need for cybersecurity standards and best practices that address interoperability, usability and privacy has been shown to be critical for the nation. NIST's cybersecurity programs seek to enable greater development and application of practical, innovative security technologies and methodologies that enhance the country's ability to address current and future computer and information security challenges.

The cybersecurity publications produced by NIST cover a wide range of cybersecurity concepts that are carefully designed to work together to produce a holistic approach to cybersecurity primarily for government agencies and constitute the best practices used by industry. This holistic strategy to cybersecurity covers the gamut of security subjects from development of secure encryption standards for communication and storage of information while at rest to how best to recover from a cyber-attack.

Why buy a book you can download for free?   We print this so you don't have to.

Some are available only in electronic media. Some online docs are missing pages or barely legible.

We at 4th Watch Publishing are former government employees, so we know how government employees actually use the standards. When a new standard is released, an engineer prints it out, punches holes and puts it in a 3-ring binder. While this is not a big deal for a 5 or 10-page document, many NIST documents are over 100 pages and printing a large document is a time-consuming effort. So, an engineer that's paid $75 an hour is spending hours simply printing out the tools needed to do the job. That's time that could be better spent doing engineering. We publish these documents so engineers can focus on what they were hired to do – engineering. It's much more cost-effective to just order the latest version from Amazon.com

If there is a standard you would like published, let us know. Our web site is usgovpub.com

Many of our titles are available as ePubs for Kindle, iPad, Nook, remarkable, BOOX, and Sony eReaders.

Why buy an eBook when you can access data on a website for free? HYPERLINKS

Yes, many books are available as a PDF, but not all PDFs are bookmarked? Do you really want to search a 6,500-page PDF document manually? Load our copy onto your Kindle, PC, iPad, Android Tablet, Nook, or iPhone (download the FREE kindle App from the APP Store) and you have an easily searchable copy. Most devices will allow you to easily navigate an ePub to any Chapter. Note that there is a distinction between a Table of Contents and "Page Navigation". Page Navigation refers to a different sort of Table of Contents. Not one appearing as a page in the book, but one that shows up on the device itself when the reader accesses the navigation feature. Readers can click on a navigation link to jump to a Chapter or Subchapter. Once there, most devices allow you to "pinch and zoom" in or out to easily read the text. (Unfortunately, downloading the free sample file at Amazon.com does not include this feature. You have to buy a copy to get that functionality, but as inexpensive as eBooks are, it's worth it.) Kindle allows you to do word search and Page Flip (temporary place holder takes you back when you want to go back and check something). Visit **www.usgovpub.com** to learn more.

NISTIR 8214

Threshold Schemes for Cryptographic Primitives

Challenges and Opportunities in Standardization and Validation of Threshold Cryptography

Luís T. A. N. Brandão
Nicky Mouha
Apostol Vassilev

This publication is available free of charge from:
https://doi.org/10.6028/NIST.IR.8214

NISTIR 8214

Threshold Schemes for Cryptographic Primitives

Challenges and Opportunities in Standardization and Validation of Threshold Cryptography

Luís T. A. N. Brandão
Nicky Mouha
Apostol Vassilev

Computer Security Division
Information Technology Laboratory

This publication is available free of charge from:
https://doi.org/10.6028/NIST.IR.8214

March 2019

U.S. Department of Commerce
Wilbur L. Ross, Jr., Secretary

National Institute of Standards and Technology
Walter G. Copan, NIST Director and Under Secretary of Commerce for Standards and Technology

National Institute of Standards and Technology Internal Report 8214
63 pages (March 2019)

This publication is available free of charge from:
https://doi.org/10.6028/NIST.IR.8214

Comments on this publication may be submitted to:

National Institute of Standards and Technology
Attn: Computer Security Division, Information Technology Laboratory
100 Bureau Drive (Mail Stop 8930) Gaithersburg, MD 20899-8930
Email: threshold-crypto@nist.gov

All comments are subject to release under the Freedom of Information Act (FOIA).

Reports on Computer Systems Technology

The Information Technology Laboratory (ITL) at the National Institute of Standards and Technology (NIST) promotes the U.S. economy and public welfare by providing technical leadership for the Nation's measurement and standards infrastructure. ITL develops tests, test methods, reference data, proof of concept implementations, and technical analyses to advance the development and productive use of information technology. ITL's responsibilities include the development of management, administrative, technical, and physical standards and guidelines for the cost-effective security and privacy of other than national security-related information in federal information systems.

Abstract

The Computer Security Division at the National Institute of Standards and Technology is interested in promoting the security of implementations of cryptographic primitives. This security depends not only on the theoretical properties of the primitives but also on the ability to withstand attacks on their implementations. It is thus important to mitigate breakdowns that result from differences between ideal and real implementations of cryptographic algorithms.

This document overviews the possibility of implementing cryptographic primitives using threshold schemes, where multiple components contribute to the operation in a way that attains the desired security goals even if f out of n of its components are compromised. There is also an identified potential in providing resistance against side-channel attacks, which exploit inadvertent leakage from real implementations. Security goals of interest include the secrecy of cryptographic keys, as well as enhanced integrity and availability, among others.

This document considers challenges and opportunities related to standardization of threshold schemes for cryptographic primitives. It includes examples illustrating security tradeoffs under variations of system model and adversaries. It enumerates several high-level characterizing features of threshold schemes, including the types of threshold, the communication interfaces (with the environment and between components), the executing platform (e.g., single device vs. multiple devices) and the setup and maintenance requirements.

The document poses a number of questions, motivating aspects to take into account when considering standardization. A particular challenge is the development of criteria that may help guide a selection of threshold cryptographic schemes. An open question is deciding at what level each standard should be defined (e.g., specific base techniques vs. conceptualized functionalities) and which flexibility of parametrization they should allow. Suitability to testing and validation of implementations are also major concerns to be addressed. Overall, the document intends to support discussion about standardization, including motivating an engagement from stakeholders. This is a step towards enabling threshold cryptography within the US federal government and beyond.

Keywords: threshold schemes; secure implementations; cryptographic primitives; threshold cryptography; secure multi-party computation; intrusion tolerance; distributed systems; resistance to side-channel attacks; standards and validation.

Acknowledgments

The authors thank their NIST colleagues who reviewed recent or early versions of this document. This includes Lily Chen, René Peralta, Ray Perlner, and Andrew Regenscheid.

The initial draft of this report was published online on July 26, 2018, for a period of public comments. We have since then received valuable feedback from external reviewers, which allowed us to improve the quality of the final document. We thank the comments received (in chronological order) from the following persons: Svetla Nikova from KU Leuven; Gokhan Kocak from Asena Inc.; Oliver Stengele from the Karlsruhe Institute of Technology; Aivo Kalu from Cybernetica AS; Christian Cachin, Hugo Krawczyk, Tal Rabin, Jason Resch and Chrysa Stathatkopoulou from IBM Research; Tanja Lange from Technische Universiteit Eindhoven; Yehuda Lindel from Bar-Ilan University and Unbound Tech; Samuel Ranellucci from Unbound Tech; Dan Bogdanov from Cybernetica AS; Rosario Gennaro from The City College of New York; Thalia May Laing from HP Labs; Karim Eldefrawy from SRI International; John Wallrabenstein from Analog.

Executive Summary

As cryptography becomes ubiquitous, it becomes increasingly relevant to address the potentially disastrous breakdowns resulting from differences between ideal and real implementations of cryptographic algorithms. These differences give rise to a range of attacks that exploit vulnerabilities in order to compromise diverse aspects of real-world implementations. Threshold schemes have the potential to enable secure modes of operation even when certain subsets of components are compromised. However, they also present new challenges for the standardization and validation of security assertions about their implementations.

This report is focused on threshold cryptographic schemes, i.e., threshold schemes used for secure implementations of cryptographic primitives. In a threshold scheme, some security property is tolerant to the compromise of up to a threshold number f (out of a total number n of) components in the system. The topic is related to traditional "threshold cryptography" (here adopted as an umbrella term), secure multi-party computation and intrusion-tolerant distributed systems. A major goal is enhanced protection of secret keys used by implementations of cryptographic algorithms. More generally, the goal includes the enhancement of a variety of security properties, such as confidentiality, integrity and/or availability.

Secret sharing is a fundamental technique in threshold cryptography. It enables a key (or some other secret input) to be split into multiple shares distributed across multiple parties. The "threshold" property translates into the ability to reconstruct the key from a threshold number of shares, but not from fewer. Thus, splitting a key into shares is an approach for protecting the secrecy of a key at rest, since the leakage of one or few shares does not reveal the key. However, this does not solve the problem of how to execute an algorithm that depends on a key. Particularly, conventional implementations of key-based cryptographic algorithms require the whole key as input, so if the key had been subject to secret sharing then the shared key would have to be reconstructed for use by the algorithm.

In threshold cryptography, the shares of the key do not need to be recombined to compute a particular result. Instead, the parties independently or collaboratively calculate shares of the output, without revealing the input shares to one another. This may be facilitated by certain mathematical properties, such as homomorphisms, or by cryptographic "secure computation" protocols. Using the threshold property, the output from the share computation can then be reconstructed into a final output. This is possible to achieve for NIST-approved algorithms, such as Rivest–Shamir–Adleman (RSA) and Digital Signature Algorithm (DSA) signatures, and Advanced Encryption Standard (AES) enciphering and deciphering.

Threshold schemes can be used, with different security goals, in different applications. For example: (i) implement a digital signature algorithm without any single component ever holding the signing key; (ii) implement encryption and decryption correctly even if one compromised component attempts to corrupt the output; (iii) generate unbiased randomness even if some (but not all) randomness contributors are biased or unavailable.

The computational paradigm in threshold cryptography brings several security advantages but also some potential weaknesses. For example, the use of multiple shares increases the attack surface to encompass all shares. Thus, the security effect of implementing a threshold scheme depends on an attack model. It is particularly relevant to consider how difficult it may be to compromise more than the threshold number f of components. In some cases, for example with low f, the increased attack surface may enable an attack more efficient and effective than possible against a conventional (non-threshold) primitive, even if the nodes in the threshold scheme have independent modes of compromise (e.g., each compromisable via mutually exclusive attack vectors). On the other hand, a threshold scheme may provide better security even if the components are individually easier to compromise, e.g., in some settings/models where they are also easier to patch.

The security effect of a threshold design may also be different across different properties of interest. For example, while the compromise of one share might not reveal the original key, the corruption of a single share (or of a computation dependent on it) may affect the integrity of the output. These observations highlight the need to look at the security benefits brought by each threshold scheme as a possible tradeoff across properties. In some settings there may be a strengthening of some security properties while for others the assurance may be reduced.

There are techniques designed to mitigate foreseen compromises in more complicated scenarios. For example, verifiable secret-sharing enables detection of misuse of shares by a shareholder, thereby enabling operational modes that tolerate this kind of corruption. As another example, proactive secret sharing can be used to periodically reshare a secret, thereby periodically reducing to zero the number of compromised shares. Assuming that old uncompromised shares are erased, the refreshing makes it more difficult to reach a state where the number of contemporaneous compromised shares surpasses the compromise threshold.

Separating the analysis of different security aspects can sometimes lead to pitfalls. To avoid such problems it is important to use appropriate formal models of security. At the same time, it is relevant to assess potential tradeoffs that a threshold cryptographic scheme induces across different security properties. A system model is also important to characterize different types of attack that a system may be subject to. Specific attacks in the real world exploit differences between conventional implementations and their idealized versions. Threshold schemes can be used to improve resistance against some of these specific attacks that breach specific security properties (e.g., confidentiality of a key) or sets thereof.

An abstract security model is not enough to assess the effects of placing a threshold scheme in an adversarial environment. One also needs to characterize implementation aspects whose variation may affect security. Such characterization helps distinguish, possibly across different application contexts, the resistance provided against certain classes of attacks. *To this end, this document proposes that a basis for discussion and comparison of threshold schemes should include the description of several characterizing features. These include the types of threshold, the communication interfaces, the target computing platforms, and the setup and maintenance requirements.*

The examples in the document illustrate how security properties can vary depending on high-level features, on assumed attack vectors and on the type of adversarial goals and capabilities. On one hand, this helps prevent a possible misconception that a higher threshold directly means higher security. On the other hand, it also intends to convey that threshold schemes can be used to implement cryptographic primitives in a more secure way. Altogether, structured security assertions also promote a path for meaningful security validation of actual implementations.

This document considers the benefits of standardizing threshold cryptographic schemes, possibly along with auxiliary threshold-cryptography primitives. Naturally, there is interest on threshold schemes for NIST-approved cryptographic primitives. Also of major importance is the development of corresponding approaches for validation of implementations of threshold cryptographic schemes. This should be aligned with the current modernization process and evolving structure of the testing methodology of the NIST cryptographic validation programs. Of particular relevance is the development of approaches to enable automated validation tests with state-of-the-art techniques.

The use of well-characterized threshold schemes to implement cryptographic primitives offers potential security benefits. But what criteria should one use to select from a potential pool of candidate threshold schemes? What flexibility of features and parameters should a threshold-cryptographic-scheme standard allow? Should some base primitives be independently standardized and/or validated? This document does not offer definitive answers to these questions. Instead, it motivates the need to develop an objective basis for addressing them. It also hints at various representative questions to consider, namely about security assessment, efficiency and applicability, among others.

There are important challenges and opportunities related to the standardization of threshold cryptographic schemes. Addressing these may bring about important security improvements to real implementations of cryptographic primitives. Fortunately, there is a plethora of research work done in the broad area of threshold cryptography, providing useful insights about possible options, caveats and tradeoffs. Further value can arise from addressing these challenges with feedback and collaboration from stakeholders, including academic researchers, industry participants and government representatives.

Table of Contents

List of Figures

List of Tables

1 Introduction

Protecting sensitive information from unauthorized disclosure has always been challenging. "Two may keep counsel, putting one away," William Shakespeare wrote in "Romeo and Juliet" (1597) [Sha97]. Later, in "Poor Richard's Almanack — 1735" [Sau34], Benjamin Franklin observed that "Three may keep a secret, if two of them are dead." Today, cryptography is a primary means of protecting digital information. In modern cryptography the algorithms are well known but the keys are secret. Thus, the effectiveness of encrypting data hinges on maintaining the secrecy of cryptographic keys. However, this is difficult in conventional implementations, as keys are usually stored in one place on a device, and used there to run the algorithm. Devices, much like people, are not completely dependable guardians of secrets. Does this mean that keys are the *Achilles' heel* of cryptography?[1]

The localization of a key, for use by an algorithm, is susceptible to enabling leaking it out. For example, the internal state of a conventional implementation might be compromised through a bug such as Heartbleed [DLK$^+$14, NVD14], Spectre [KGG$^+$18, NVD18a, NVD18b], Meltdown [LSG$^+$18, NVD18c] and Foreshadow [BMW$^+$18], letting an attacker read private memory locations, including secret keys contained therein. Another example is the cold-boot attack [HSH$^+$09], which allows recovery of keys from the dynamic random access memory (DRAM) of a computer, even seconds to minutes after it has been removed from the device. Some attacks inject faults into the computation, for example by changing the supply voltage. An example is the "Bellcore" attack [BDL97, ABF$^+$03], where a fault induces an incorrect computation whose output reveals a secret key. Other attacks obtain information through a side channel, such as the execution time, the amount of energy it consumes, or the electromagnetic emanations it produces. Many of these fall into the category of non-invasive attacks, which can be performed without direct physical contact with components within the device. Attacks that exploit leakage of key-dependent information can lead to disastrous scenarios in which the master key used to encrypt and authenticate device firmware becomes compromised [RSWO17].

To counter the inherent security risks of handling secret keys in conventional implementations of cryptographic algorithms, technical approaches have emerged that split the secret key into two or more shares across different components or parties. For example, when secret sharing is used on the key, the compromise of up to the confidentiality threshold number f (out of n) of the shares does not reveal information about the original key. Using appropriate threshold techniques, the shares can then be separately processed, leading the computation to a correct result as if the original secret key had been processed by a classic algorithm. The threshold approach can thus significantly increase the confidentiality of secret keys in cryptographic implementations.

There is a potential benefit complementary to mitigating single-point-of-failure issues in hardware and software implementations. The threshold approach can also enable decen-

---

[1] Some portions of writing were adapted from text appearing at a previous short magazine article [VMB18].

tralization of trust, when delegating the ability to perform some cryptographic operation. This can be useful for higher-level distributed applications, e.g., when the performing of a cryptographic operation should require agreement by multiple parties.

This report is focused on threshold schemes applied to cryptographic primitives. In an f-out-of-n threshold scheme, some security property is tolerant to some kind of compromise of up to f out of n components in the system. As a mnemonic, the symbol f can be thought of as counting the number of "**f**aulty" (i.e., compromised) components that can be tolerated. This threshold f can be specific to some implicit type of compromise, e.g., possibly including cases of crash, leakage, intrusion and accidental or malicious malfunctioning.

In a dual perspective, a threshold can be defined with respect to an operational property. A k-out-of-n threshold property denotes that the presence or participation of k correct components is required to ensure some correct operation. The relation between the different thresholds (respectively represented by symbols k and f), e.g., $k = f + 1$ or $k = 2f + 1$, can vary depending on the scheme and on the type of compromise and security property.

The threshold paradigm brings several security advantages but also some potential weaknesses. For example, the use of multiple shares increases the attack surface to encompass all shares. Thus, the security effect of implementing a threshold scheme depends on an attack model. It is particularly relevant to consider how difficult may be the compromise of more than the threshold number f of components. In some cases, for example with low f, the increased attack surface may enable an attack more efficient and effective than possible against a conventional (non-threshold) primitive.

The threshold concept can apply to security properties of interest beyond the secrecy of keys. For example, it is useful to enable availability and integrity of computations in spite of malfunctioning of some of its components. Traditional techniques of fault tolerance often achieve such resistance when considering random or predictably modeled faults. However, we are specially interested in resistance against targeted attacks, which can be malicious and arbitrary. Considering a wide scope of security goals, threshold schemes can exist in several flavors, depending on the security aspects they address and the techniques used. There are challenges in ensuring the simultaneous upholding of diverse security properties, such as secrecy of key material, correctness of outputs and continued availability.

In fact, the security impact of a threshold design may be different across different properties of interest. For example, in some schemes the compromise of one share might not reveal the original key, but the corruption of a single share (or of a computation dependent on it) may affect the integrity of the output. These observations highlight the need to look at the security benefits brought by threshold cryptography as a possible tradeoff across properties.

The basic security model for cryptographic algorithms assumes an ideal black box, in which the cryptographic computations are correct and the internal states are kept secret. For example, such ideal constructs have no side channels that could leak secret keys. This model contrasts with the reality of conventional implementations, which can be subject to attacks that exploit differences between the ideal and real worlds. Threshold schemes deal with some of those differences, by providing tolerance against the compromise of several components. They may also hinder the exploitation of existing compromises (such as noisy leakage) from a set of components, e.g., providing resistance against side-channel attacks.

A separate analysis of different security properties may lead to some pitfalls. Some formal models of security are useful to avoid them. The ideal-real simulation paradigm, common to analysis of secure multi-party computation protocols, combines the notion of security into a definition of an ideal world. This abstraction captures an intended application in an ideal world, then allowing security properties to be derived therefrom. Complementary, a system model is also important to characterize different types of attack that a system may be subject to. Specific attacks in the real world exploit differences between conventional implementations and their idealized versions. Some of these may target breaching specific security properties (e.g., confidentiality of a key) or sets thereof. There is a particular interest in understanding how threshold schemes can be used to improve resistance against these specific attacks. It is also relevant to assess potential tradeoffs that a threshold cryptographic scheme induces across different security properties.

There are techniques designed to mitigate foreseen compromises in more complicated scenarios. For example, verifiable secret-sharing enables detection of misuse of shares by a shareholder, thereby enabling operational modes that tolerate this kind of corruption. As another example, proactive secret sharing can be used to periodically reshare a secret, thereby periodically reducing to zero the number of compromised shares. However, an abstract security model is not enough to assess the effects of placing a threshold scheme in an adversarial environment. One also needs to characterize implementation aspects whose variation may affect security. These include the types of threshold, the communication interfaces, the target computing platforms, and the setup and maintenance requirements.

For example, system models and attack types can differ substantially across different platforms and communication mediums. It should thus be considered how the components inter-communicate, and how they can be assumed separate and independent vs. mutually interfering. In a single device setting, this may involve interaction between different components within a single chip or a single computer. In a contrasting setting, multiple nodes (e.g., servers) may be placed in different locations, communicating within a private network or across the Internet.

Altogether, the security assertions made with respect to an instantiated set of features provide a path for security validation of actual implementations. Of particular interest are approaches that enable automated validation tests with state-of-the-art techniques. The use of well-characterized threshold cryptographic schemes to implement cryptographic primitives offers potential security benefits. It is thus important to develop objective criteria for selecting from a potential pool of candidate threshold schemes.

Audience. This document is targeted, with varying goals, at a diverse audience. Internally for NIST, the goal is to initiate a discussion about threshold schemes for cryptographic primitives. This motivated the inclusion of representative questions relevant to standardization.

The document is also written for people with managerial/policy responsibilities in development and/or adoption of cryptographic services and modules. For such an audience, the document highlights critical aspects of the security of implementations that can be significantly affected by nuances in the system model and the employed threshold techniques. Several simple examples are provided, including some based on classic secret sharing schemes.

The text is also directed to experts in cryptography from academia and industry. For them, the document is an invitation to engage with NIST in a collaborative effort to resolve the open questions related to the standardization of threshold schemes for cryptographic primitives and the corresponding guidelines for implementation validation.

It is useful to further clarify one intentional design aspect related to the references to related work. This document intends to initiate a discussion that may lead NIST to standardize threshold schemes for cryptographic primitives. For that purpose, we sought to convey in a balanced way that there are feasible threshold approaches, but without showing particular preferences. In fact, we specifically opted to avoid an assessment of the most recent works, preferring instead to exemplify precursory threshold techniques. Therefore, we do not make an exhaustive analysis and do not try to include the depth and nuances typical of a research paper or a technical survey. We hope that a thorough assessment of state-of-the-art threshold approaches can be subsequently performed with an inclusive participation of stakeholders.

2   Fundamentals

2.1   Terminology

This document makes use of two dual perspectives of a threshold. In "f-out-of-n" the threshold "f" denotes the *maximum* number of components that can be *compromised* (with respect to some implicit security property of the components), while retaining some (implicit) security property for the global system. Correspondingly, in "k-out-of-n" the threshold "k" denotes the *minimum* number of components that must remain *uncompromised* to be possible to ensure some security property of the global system.

We borrow terminology from different research areas, with some overlap, using several terms that share similar connotations, sometimes (but not always) interchangeable. Some informal correspondences follow:

- **Active/byzantine/malicious**: characterization of compromised nodes, or of an adversary, when being able to arbitrarily deviate or induce deviations from a protocol specification.

- **Agent/component/node/party/share**: a constituent part of an implemented threshold scheme, affecting the prosecution of a functional goal (a cryptographic operation, in our context) to be achieved by a collective of parts; most often used to denote one of the n parts whose compromise counts towards the threshold f; when the context is clear, some terms can designate parts outside of the threshold composition.

- **Aggregator/broker/combiner/dealer/proxy/relay**: an agent with a special role in aiding the setup, execution and/or maintenance of a threshold protocol; usually not accounted in n, except if explicitly stated as such (e.g., the case of a primary node).

- **Bad/compromised/corrupted/controlled/faulty/intruded**: state of a node, whereby it departs from an ideally healthy state, and starts being counted towards the threshold f.

- **Client/user**: an agent, not in the threshold set of components, who is a stakeholder of the result of a cryptographic computation, typically the requester for that computation.

- **Compromise/corruption/intrusion**: a process by which a node transitions from an ideally healthy state to a compromised state and/or by which it remains therein.

- **Good/healthy/honest/recovered**: ideal state of a node, not yet compromised by an adversary, but susceptible to attacks.

- **Honest-but-curious/Leaky/Passive/Semi-honest**: characterization of compromised components, or of an adversary, when the internal state of the former is exfiltrated by the latter, but without altering the computations and message-exchanges specified by the protocol.

- **Recovery/refresh/rejuvenation/replacement**: transitioning of a node or nodes from a (possibly) bad state back to a good state; nuances include update, reversion, change and reset of internal states, as well as effective replacement of physical components.

The above notes simply intend to convey intuition helpful for reading the document. We do not undertake here the goal of unifying terminology from different areas. Cited references in the text provide necessary context. The encyclopedia of cryptography and security [TJ11] and the NIST glossary of security terms [Kis13] provide additional suggestions.

2.2 Secret sharing

Secret sharing is based on splitting the key into multiple shares. For example, to split key K into three shares K_1, K_2, and K_3, we randomly select shares K_1 and K_2 from the same key space as K, and let the third share $K_3 = K_1 \oplus K_2 \oplus K$ be the one-time pad encryption of K, where $\oplus$ is the exclusive OR operation if the keys are bit-strings. No two shares provide any information about the secret key — all shares are required to recover K.

The described scheme, with $n = 3$ parties, has a threshold property: it is a "f-out-of-3" scheme with $f = 2$ with respect to the leakage of any two shares alone not giving away information of the original secret key; it is a k-out-of-3 scheme with $k = 3$ with respect to all three shares being required to recover the key. The k notation is used hereafter for the concrete case of secret-sharing schemes.

More generally, k-out-of-n secret-sharing schemes can be defined, for any integers n and k satisfying $n \geq k \geq 1$. Such secret-sharing schemes were independently developed in 1979 by Shamir [Sha79] and Blakley [Bla79]. There, any k parties together can recover a secret shared across n parties, but $k-1$ parties together do not know anything about the secret.

Blakley secret sharing.   With the help of Fig. 1, we describe an example of Blakley's scheme for $k = 2$ and $n = 3$, with some simplifications for illustration purposes. The secret is the x-coordinate (x_s) of the point $P(x, y)$ in the two-dimensional plane (see Fig. 1(a)). A non-vertical line in the plane is defined as a set of points (x, y) satisfying $y = hx + g$ for some constants h and g. If Alice obtains coefficients h_A and g_A for some line $\{(x, y) : y = h_A x + g_A\}$, containing the point P, this does not give Alice any advantage in discovering its x-coordinate x_s (see Fig. 1(b)). This is because the definition of the line does not provide any special information about any point in the line, i.e. all points in the line (and all x-coordinates) are equally likely. In practice, lines are selected only from a finite space of lines, e.g., with all coefficients being integers modulo some prime number Q, and the lines themselves are finite collections of points, e.g., with x and y being also integers modulo Q. The prime modulus Q must be larger than the secret x_s and larger than the number n of parties.

Similarly, if Bob and Charlie obtain coefficients of other lines that pass through the same point P, individually they cannot determine P. Note that the lines cannot be parallel to each other and to Alice's line. However, any two together — Alice with Bob, or Alice with Charlie, or Bob with Charlie — can easily compute P as the intersection of their lines (see Fig. 1(c)). We have thus described a 2-out-of-3 secret-sharing scheme. To build a k-out-of-n Blakley scheme for some $k > 2$, one considers hyperplanes $y = h_1 x_1 + ... + h_{k-1} x_{k-1} + g$ that intersect in a single point $P(x_1, ..., x_{k-1}, y)$ in the k-dimensional space, provided that no hyper-place is orthogonal to the x_1-axis. Choosing $n \geq k$ such hyperplanes, one can distribute the corresponding coefficients to n different parties. Then any k parties together can compute efficiently the intersection point P and recover the secret as its x_1-coordinate.

Shamir secret sharing.   Shamir secret sharing is based on the observation that any set of k distinct points determines completely a polynomial of degree $k-1$. For example, consider a set of positive integer coefficients $c_0, c_1, ..., c_{k-1}$ and define the polynomial $f(x) = c_0 + c_1 x + ... + c_{k-1} x^{k-1}$. Typically, the secret is the coefficient $c_0 = f(0)$ and each party i receives as share the point $(i, f(i))$, where i is a positive integer distinct for each party (e.g., $1, 2, ..., n$). Then, any set of k parties can reconstruct $f(x)$, and therefore compute the secret $f(0)$, whereas $k-1$ parties cannot. All coefficients are based on finite field arithmetic defined in terms of a prime number Q. Since each party must receive a distinct point, and that point must not be $(0, f(0))$, the modulus Q must be larger than the number n of parties. The points on the curve are thus defined as $(x, f(x) \bmod Q)$ and the secret and any other

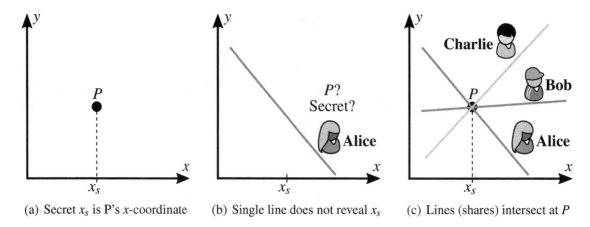

(a) Secret x_s is P's x-coordinate   (b) Single line does not reveal x_s (c) Lines (shares) intersect at P

Figure 1. Illustration[2] of Blakley secret sharing

coefficient are integers between 0 and $Q - 1$. This ensures that no information from the secret can be recovered from incomplete sets of (i.e., with fewer than k) points on the curve.

The schemes of Shamir and Blakley are information-theoretically secure, which means that in a standalone set of $k - 1$ shares there is indeed no information about the secret.

While information-theoretic security may be an advantage, the property requires that each share is of the same size as the secret, thus meaning that the overall size of all shares is n times the size of the secret. In contrast, there are secret-sharing schemes with reduced optimal size, at the cost of guaranteeing only computational (i.e., cryptographic) security [Kra94]. There, the size of each share can be up to k times smaller than the size of the secret — this is especially useful if secret sharing is to be used to share large amounts of data.

Note: some elements of secret-sharing are standardized by the International Organization for Standardization (ISO) / International Electrotechnical Commission (IEC) [ISO16, ISO17].

2.3 Secret resharing

The need to compute new random shares for the same original secret key often arises in practice. It may happen that over time some $(< k)$ shares are compromised [OY91], thus creating a need to compute new shares and discard the old ones. Resharing can even be proactive [HJKY95], e.g., at regular intervals in time and not as a direct response to a detected compromise.

Resharing in Blakley's scheme. We continue here the 2-out-of-3 example of Blakley's scheme, where two parties are required to reconstruct a secret x_s shared among three parties. Each resharing of x_s requires re-randomizing the point P along the vertical line that defines

---

[2] The humanoid cliparts are from clker.com/clipart-*.html, where * is 2478, 2482 and 2479.

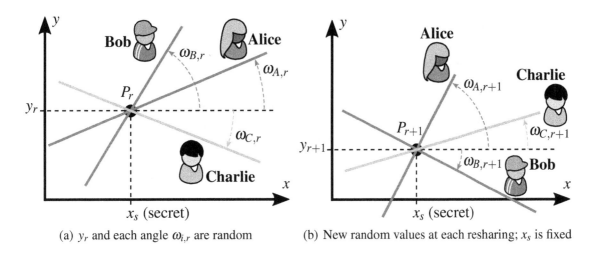

(a) y_r and each angle $\omega_{i,r}$ are random   (b) New random values at each resharing; x_s is fixed

Figure 2. Illustration of share randomization in Blakley secret sharing

the secret. In other words, for each randomization iteration r a random y-coordinate y_r is sampled, defining a new point $P_r = (x_s, y_r)$. Then, the new share (a line) for each party is also randomized, subject to the constraints that all new lines are non-vertical, intersect at the new point P_r and are different from one another. With this construction, a single party (Alice, Bob, or Charlie) still cannot gain any useful insight into the reshared secret x_s. This is because at each new resharing r the point P_r where the three lines intersect is chosen randomly in the vertical line that passes through the secret.

For visual intuition, we illustrate in Fig. 2 a parametrization based on angles. A line through a point P in the plane can be parametrized in terms of its angle ω, in the interval $(-\pi/2, \pi/2)$, with respect to the x axis. Thus, for each resharing iteration r we attribute to each party i a new random angle $w_{i,r}$ and the x-coordinate where the line intersects with the x-axis. In practice the used parametrization is based on polynomial coefficients, so the share (a line) is instead revealed as (g, h), where $y = hx + g$ is the equation that defines the line.

For each new iteration $r + 1$, one computes a new point $P_{r+1} = (x_s, y_{r+1})$ and new random lines for each party. These lines, passing through point P_{r+1} correspond to new random angles, as illustrated in Fig. 2(b). The party selecting new shares must ensure that the lines of different parties do not overlap, i.e., that they do not have the same angles, and are non-vertical. Concretely, this means that $\omega_{i,r} \neq \omega_{j,r} \neq \pi/2$ for $i, j \in \{A, B, C\}$ and $i \neq j$. The generalization to the case $k > 2$ is as before: the new point P would require randomizing $k - 1$ coordinates, and the resharing would proceed as in the initial sharing.

Resharing in Shamir's scheme.   Share re-randomization can also be done with Shamir secret sharing. There, the fixed secret is $c_0 \bmod Q = f(0) \bmod Q$. At each randomization iteration r, one chooses random coefficients $c_{1,r}, ..., c_{k-1,r}$ for a new polynomial $f_r(x) = c_0 + c_{1,r}x + ... + c_{k-1,r}x^{k-1}$ satisfying $f_r(0) = c_0$. The new shares are then points evaluated with f_r. Concretely, each party i, for $i = 1, 2, 3, ...$ receives $f_r(i)$ as its new share.

2.4   Threshold cryptography

We take broad input from several research areas with traditionally distinctive names, but with a strong relation to threshold schemes. Since we are focused on the implementation of cryptographic primitives, we adopt the umbrella term "threshold cryptography" to denote our area of interest. The expression "threshold cryptography" has been traditionally used to refer to schemes where some computation is performed over secret shares of inputs [DF90, DSDFY94]. Usually, the setting is such that the shares are used to compute something useful, but without being revealed across parties. Often, a main security goal is secrecy of cryptographic keys, but a variety of other security properties, such as integrity and availability, may also be a motivating drive. Achieving these properties is possible based on a variety of techniques. For example, integrity may in some settings be enhanced based on verifiable secret sharing schemes [AMGC85, Fel87] and/or zero-knowledge proofs [GMR85, BFM88], allowing checking whether shares are used consistently. Specifically, a threshold scheme can be made robust against adversarially induced inconsistencies in shares or in related computations, outputting correct results in spite of up to a threshold number of compromised parties [GRJK00]. While we focus on secure implementations of cryptographic primitives, the actual threshold techniques may also include non-cryptographic techniques, e.g., simple replication and majority voting.

One main area of related research is "secure multi-party computation" (SMPC) [Yao86, GMW87, BGW88, CCD88]. It allows mutually distrustful parties to compute functions (and randomized functionalities) of their combined inputs, without revealing the corresponding inputs to one another. This can be useful for threshold schemes even if the inputs of different parties are not shares of some key and/or if the actual computation requires interaction between parties. Provided suitable definitions and assumptions, any cryptographic primitive can be implemented in a threshold manner based on SMPC. Often this is based on a framework of definitions of ideal functionalities, and protocols that emulate those functionalities. Nonetheless, some systems may implement threshold techniques (e.g., secret-sharing, replication) not modeled within an SMPC framework.

Threshold schemes also do not encompass all that exists in the realm of SMPC. In usual SMPC descriptions, the parties themselves are stakeholders of the secrecy of their input and correctness of the output, e.g., in the millionaires' problem [Yao82] and in secure set intersection [FNP04]. In threshold schemes for cryptographic primitives, the nodes within the threshold system can have a neutral interest for the outcome, and in fact just be a service provider (of cryptographic services) to a set of external users/clients.

Threshold schemes can also be based on elements from the "distributed systems" research area, where fault and intrusion tolerance are main topics. Common properties of interest in distributed systems are liveness (making progress even in the face of concurrent execution/requests) and safety (ensuring consistency of state across multiple parties). Why would this be relevant for threshold cryptography? As an example, consider implementing a multi-party threshold version of a full-fledged cryptographic platform. Such a platform would perform a variety of cryptographic operations, some using secret keys, and based on requests by users whose credentials and authorization profiles may be updated across time. Now we could ask: in a setting where *availability* (of cryptographic operations) is a critical property, and where the system is supposed to operate even in cases of network *partition* (i.e., even if some parties in the threshold scheme cannot inter-communicate), can *consistency* (of state, e.g., credentials, across different parties) be simultaneously satisfied under concurrent executions? This is a kind of "distributed systems" problem relevant for threshold schemes. There are settings [Bre12] where these three properties (consistency, availability and partition tolerance) cannot be guaranteed to be achieved simultaneously.

2.5 Side-channel and fault attacks

The secrecy of keys can be compromised by the leakage of key-dependent information during computations. This is possible even without direct physical contact with components within the device. For example, the time taken, the power consumed, and the electromagnetic radiation emanated by a device can be measured without penetrating the device enclosure.

We will assume that, regardless of whether the computation is in hardware or software, the device that performs the computation consists of some circuit with wires connecting to logical gates and memory cells. Then, the attacker's view of the circuit elements may be noisy (the *noisy leakage* model [CJRR99]), or the attacker may be limited by the number of wires of the circuit that it can observe within a certain period of time (the *probing* model [ISW03]). The noisy leakage model and probing model have been unified [DDF14]. In both models, under some reasonable assumptions on the statistical distributions of side-channel information, the complexity of a side-channel attack of a suitable implementation with an n-out-of-n secret-sharing increases exponentially with the number of shares.

As such, side channel attacks on secret-shared implementations become infeasible if the number of shares is sufficiently high, and is further thwarted when the shares are refreshed before the attacker can collect enough side-channel information. Further refinements of the model take transient behavior ("glitches") of the transistors into account, which can be handled by Threshold Implementations (TI) [NRR06] or by "lazy engineering" to just increase the number of shares [BGG$^+$14].

Besides the aforementioned side-channel attacks, an attacker may also obtain key-dependent information by injecting a fault into the computation, and then observing the outputs [BDL97]. To inject the fault, the attacker may, for example, apply a strong external electromagnetic field. Note that the injection of faults may also introduce errors in the outputs of the computation, thereby violating the integrity of the outputs. If the threshold scheme is endowed with the ability to detect which shares have errors, and if the threshold scheme does not require all shares to be present, it can resist temporary and permanent faults in parts of the computation. This would provide resistance against a wide range of fault attacks.

3   Examples

3.1   Threshold signature examples

3.1.1   Basic threshold computation on secret shares

First, we recall the RSA (Rivest-Shamir-Adleman) signature scheme [RSA78], which defines the public key as (N, e) and the private key as d, such that $ed = 1 \bmod \phi(N)$. Here, the modulus N is a product of two large secret primes and ϕ is Euler's totient function. Then, the RSA signature for a (possibly hashed) message m is defined as $s = m^d \bmod N$. Anyone possessing the public key can verify the signature by checking $s^e = m^{ed} = m \bmod N$.

Now let us proceed to describe a simple threshold variant of this signature scheme [Fra90, BH98]. We first consider the role of a dealer — someone that, knowing the secret parameter $\phi(N)$ and the secret signing key d, wishes to delegate to other parties the ability to jointly produce signatures in a threshold manner. The dealer splits the private key d into three shares d_1, d_2, and d_3, such that $d_1 + d_2 + d_3 = d \bmod \phi(N)$. Now, without reconstructing d, it is possible to first process the message independently using each of the shares: $s_1 = m^{d_1}$, $s_2 = m^{d_2}$, and $s_3 = m^{d_3}$; and then compute the signature $s = s_1 s_2 s_3$. Note that this is indeed a valid RSA signature, as $s_1 s_2 s_3 = m^{d_1 + d_2 + d_3} = m^d \bmod N$. This simple threshold RSA signature scheme mitigates the risk of exposing the potentially high-value private key d, which does not appear in any of the three shares that are used in the actual computations. Thus, compromising any one of the shares, and even two of them, poses no threat of exposing d. Moreover, frequent updates to the key shares (d_1, d_2, and d_3) would reduce the window of opportunity for attacks and thereby further reduce the risk. Refreshing can even occur after every signature.

3.1.2   A k-out-of-n threshold scheme

In the above example, all shares must be present. This might be impractical in situations where one or more of the shares become unavailable. For such cases, a k-out-of-n threshold scheme could be used when at least k shares are available.

But how to generalize from the n-out-of-n to a k-out-of-n signature scheme (with $k < n$)? The needed secret-sharing is no longer a simple additive decomposition into shares (in the exponent), and correspondingly the combination into a final signature becomes more complex, namely because the share-holders do not know $\phi(N)$ (the *group order*). It is nonetheless possible to slightly adjust the computation of key shares and signature shares so that the final combination becomes possible even without knowledge of the secret information [Sho00]. The secret vs. public knowledge of the order of the underlying group can indeed be relevant in the development of diverse threshold schemes, with some schemes taking advantage of using groups with publicly known group order (e.g., as in the case of ElGamal decryption [DF90]).

So for RSA signatures one can use, e.g., a 2-out-of-3 secret-sharing scheme, and a corresponding threshold variant of RSA. Then, in the case of one share being irrecoverably lost or breached, the private signature key d remains intact, available, and not breached. This means that one can continue to use the same public key to verify the correctness of the signature.

In contrast, when a conventional implementation is breached, the corresponding public/private key pair would have to be revoked and a new pair issued. Typically this also requires an external certification of the public key by a certificate authority and propagating it to all relying parties. In addition, a 2-out-of-3 threshold signature scheme becomes more resilient to future share losses if it continuously refreshes the key shares, provided that at most one is compromised at any given time. Note that in a scheme composed of three separate conventional RSA implementations with independent keys, refreshing would require updating the public/private key pairs, along with all entailing inconveniences.

3.1.3   Avoiding the dealer

In the above descriptions, an implicit trusted party, often called the *dealer*, knows the secret d and performs each secret-sharing operation. Particularly, the threshold RSA examples based on a common modulus N required the dealer to also know the secret prime factorization. If needed, the dealer could, without revealing the secret, prove to each share-holder that N is indeed a valid product of two primes, by using zero-knowledge proofs [vdGP88]. Nonetheless, in a dealerless setting a threshold computation of shares of the secret signing key d would also require a threshold generation of the public N, along with a secret sharing of its factorization. This does not lend itself to a straightforward efficient computation, but can in general be done based on SMPC protocols [BF97]. Different RSA-based threshold schemes can take advantage of specialized solutions, with tradeoffs related to the threshold parameters k and n and to properties of the prime factorization.

Schemes based on particular assumptions can enable a more straightforward selection and verification of the validity of public elements. For example, this is possible based on assumptions of intractability of computing discrete logarithms in certain groups of known order. If the group parameters can be verified as correct in a standalone procedure, then no one requires having any secret knowledge about the group. Furthermore, if the selection is made in a way that avoids the possibility of a trapdoor being known, then the parameters can be trusted by anyone. The intractability assumption can then, for fixed security parameters, be accepted for global parameters of a group (e.g., [Ber06]). In particular, this can facilitate a respective threshold mechanism, so that a secret key never exists locally at any entity. For example, one can then define a dealer-absent threshold version of a public key generation (the result of an exponentiation), such that each party knows one share of the secret key (a discrete logarithm) [Ped91, GJKR99].

The same possibilities exist for resharing. In suitable threshold schemes, the share-holders can perform resharing without a dealer, i.e., interacting to create new shares for the same secret, without ever reconstructing the secret. The final shares can even be obtained for new threshold structures (e.g., different threshold and number of parties) [DJ97].

3.1.4   Other constructions

The above examples focused on threshold schemes where the secret-key is shared, and then a threshold scheme enables a generation of a signature identical to the non-threshold manner. A feature of those schemes is that the final signature is identical to a non-threshold one, thereby being inherently efficient in size (i.e., not incurring an increase with the threshold parameter). Such schemes also have the property that the identities of the signatories remain secret to the external users interested in verifying the correctness of a signature. However, some settings may favor the identifiability of signatories, e.g., as an accountability and credibility feature. Each signatory might also prefer retaining an individual public credential, not wanting to use a private-key share associated with a common public key. Even in this setting it is possible to devise short threshold signatures, with size equal to a non-threshold signature. Concretely, "multi-signature" schemes [IN83, MOR01] enable multiple parties, with independent secret-public key pairs, to jointly produce a common short signature.[3]

A multi-signature scheme can be used as a threshold signature scheme where the application layer, and possibly the user, has added *flexibility* to define which subsets of signatories determine a valid signature, i.e., beyond structures defined by a pre-determined threshold number. For example, a multi-signature may be defined as valid if it contains one signature from each of three groups of individuals in different roles in an organization. The verification procedure then depends on the set of independent public keys. For example, these schemes can be easily based on Schnorr signatures [Sch90, BN06].

To complement the resilience in the face of compromise, signatures can also be implemented with a "forward security" property [And02]. Such schemes can be based on an evolving private key, while the public key remains fixed, so that even a future key leakage will not allow the adversary to forge past messages, assuming the signer erases past keys [BM99]. To some extent, this property has some conceptual similarity to the refreshing we previously described in the RSA example. This property can be achieved also for threshold signatures [AMN01], including the case of multi-signatures [SA09].

In summary, we showed by examples that "threshold signature schemes" can be based on secret-shared computation of regular signatures or on multi-signatures, with or without a dealer, with or without robustness, and possibly with forward security.

Several of the exemplified threshold schemes take advantage of group homomorphic properties. While such properties are not applicable in every cryptographic primitive, threshold computation can still in general be obtained via secure multi-party computation.

---

[3] These should not be confused with "group signatures" [CvH91], where a member of a group signs a message, while proving group membership but remaining anonymous with respect to its identity within the group.

3.2   Side-channel attacks and countermeasures

Timing attacks were first presented by Kocher [Koc96], and have been shown to be easy to perform on a variety of cryptographic algorithms. An advantage of timing attacks is that no specialized equipment is required. Because they do not require physical access to the system, they may even be performed remotely over the Internet [BB03].

A possible countermeasure against timing attacks is to ensure that the implementation is "constant time," that is, that its execution time does not depend on the value of the secret key. This turns out to be surprisingly difficult for many commonly-used implementations. The reason is that having "constant-time" source code, that is, source code without key-dependent branches or memory accesses [Ber05], may not be sufficient. Indeed, an implementation that is free of timing attacks on one platform may be vulnerable on another platform. This can happen, for example, when source code that contains multiplication operations is compiled with a different runtime library [KPVV16], or when the same binary is executed on a different processor [Por18].

The execution time of the program, however, is just one example of a side channel. Implementations in hardware and software may also leak through other side channels, such as power consumption or electromagnetic radiation. The limitation of the currently-known countermeasures (such as "constant-time" implementations, dual-rail logic, or electromagnetic shielding) is that they usually do not get rid of all the leakage, but may still be vulnerable to higher-order or data-dependent leakages.

To protect against side-channel attacks, the framework of threshold cryptography can provide a promising starting point. If the implementation is split into a number of "parties," such that no single party holds the entire secret required to perform the cryptographic operation, then the leakage of information from only one "party" would not enable a successful attack on the original secret.

However, when all these parties reside on a single chip, we must assume that an attacker can gain *some* (bounded) information about *every* party. In that case, it may happen that the threshold cryptosystem only complicates a side-channel attack by a small factor, depending on the number of parties. For example, the n-out-of-n threshold block cipher by Brickell et al. [BCF00] uses the n-fold composition (or cascade) of a block cipher with n different keys, which may slow down power analysis attacks only by roughly a factor of n.

Nevertheless, there exist sound countermeasures against side-channel attacks where the secret variables are split into shares, such that a threshold number of shares can be used to recombine the secret, but fewer shares reveal no information at all. We described the theoretical foundation of these approaches and their resistance against side-channel attacks in Sec. 2.

4 Models

The basic security model for conventional cryptographic algorithms assumes an ideal black box, in which the cryptographic computations are correct and all internal states, including keys, are kept secret. This basic model leaves aside the possibility of leakage through side-channels, such as timing and power. This may be due to these parameters not being included in the model, or being assumed independent of the secrets (e.g., assuming instantaneous or constant-time computations). Under this assumption, the problem of quantifying a security property of the algorithm can be reduced to the problem of evaluating the complexity of the best-known attack against this model.

For example, one can define the security strength, which can also be expressed as bit strength, of different classes of cryptographic algorithms based on the amount of work needed to perform a brute-force search of the key in a large space related to the key size. When the algorithms are implemented in real hardware and software, the black-box assumption can break down in several ways. For example, bugs in the implementation can lead to side effects that compromise the secret key, as with Heartbleed. Also, the material and electromagnetic characteristics of the platforms on which the algorithms run can cause side-channel information to leak and allow attackers to recover the secret key.

The distinction of ideal versus real implementations can yield useful insights into the assessment of threshold schemes for cryptographic primitives. What are the security advantages and disadvantages of performing separate computations on shares of a key, compared to conventional implementations that use a single secret key? How can threshold cryptography mitigate the potentially disastrous consequences that a coding error or a side-channel leak could have on a conventional implementation?

This section considers how a range of applicable scenarios may differently affect a range of tradeoffs between several security properties. These scenarios depend on adversarial goals and capabilities, and various properties of the system model. It is important to be aware that security strengthening and weakening may co-exist. The discussion also preludes the next section, which motivates the need to describe characterizing features of threshold schemes.

4.1 Security considerations

In a first baseline comparison, a real implementation allows vectors of attack not possible in an ideal black-box. Once these are identified, one asks how to augment conventional implementations, in the real world, to improve security. Particularly, *how does a threshold approach affect security, compared to a non-threshold approach?* Perhaps security is improved if an attacker is limited to not compromising more than f-out-of-n components within a certain time interval. Also, as explained in Sec. 3.2, a threshold design may make it inherently more difficult to exploit existing compromises (such as noisy leakage) in the set of "parties". While these intuitions are valuable, we want to enable a more meaningful formulation and/or validation of security assertions about implementations based on threshold schemes.

Two general metrics of interest are *reliability* and *availability* [Rad97]. We can call them meta-metrics, since we are especially interested in considering them to measure (even when just qualitatively/comparatively) the upholding of concrete security properties related to implementations under attack. Reliability — probability of not failing a security goal — is specially suited for cases of "all-or-nothing" security, where the break of a certain property represents a catastrophic failure. For example, if a secret decryption key is leaked, then secrecy is lost with respect to the plaintext associated with public ciphertexts, without anything being able to revert it. Availability — proportion of time during which a security goal is satisfied — can be used to measure the actual "availability" of a service or property, e.g., the proportion of cryptographic output produced as intended. These metrics also depend on the mission time of an application, so it is relevant to consider, for example, resilience enhanced by *rejuvenating* compromised components back into a healthy state.

4.1.1 Diverse security properties

A threshold augmentation may have different effects across different security properties, e.g., confidentiality vs. availability vs. integrity, possibly improving one while degrading others. To show the nuances, consider the 3-out-of-3 threshold RSA-signature scheme described in Sec. 3.1.1, supported on a 3-out-of-3 secret sharing of the key. (Recall that, with the notation used here, a 3-out-of-3 secret sharing of the key means $k = 3$ for availability, i.e., three parties (out of $n = 3$) are necessary to produce a signature, and $f = 2$ for confidentiality, i.e., any subset of only two parties cannot learn anything about the key.) There, each node loses visibility of the original signing key, but retains the ability to influence the output of a computation dependent on the key. If a compromised node simply refrains from outputting, then it compromises the availability of the signing operation. If a corrupted node outputs a syntactically valid but semantically incorrect output share, then it may or may not compromise the integrity of the final signature, depending on whether or not the mechanism (implicit in the example) responsible for recombining the output shares is prescribed or not to verify the correctness of the signature.

In summary, even for the considered simple example of "3-out-of-3" signature scheme (based on a "3-out-of-3" secret sharing), there are different compromise thresholds for different properties. For example, the compromise thresholds for confidentiality (of the signing key) and availability (to produce signatures) are respectively $f_C = 2$ and $f_A = 0$, similar to the underlying secret-sharing scheme. For integrity of produced signatures, the compromise threshold is by default also equal to $f_I = 0$, since the described mechanism produces an incorrect signature if one of the output shares is incorrect. However, one can also consider an analysis that incorporates the context of a signature application where the corruption is detected by a verification against the provided plaintext. If the detection of a bad signature prevents an error propagation in the application, then the integrity compromise can be disregarded ($f_I = n$) and the problem be instead classified as an availability issue ($f_A = 0$). More generally, for a "k-out-of-n" signature scheme: $f_C = k - 1$ (for the confidentiality of the signing key); f_A can depend on the scheme, but ideally can be as high as $n - k$; f_I can depend on the scheme and on the application definition of integrity compromise.

Based on the above, under certain types of attack the exemplified threshold scheme may, in comparison with the conventional scheme, improve the confidentiality of the original key, while degrading the availability and/or integrity of the intended output. Particularly, this happens if: (when $f_A = 0$) compromising the availability of **one** ($= 1 + f_A$) out of the three nodes in the threshold version is easier than compromising the availability of a conventional non-threshold version; (when $f_I = 0$) if compromising the integrity of **one** ($= 1 + f_I$) out of the three nodes in the threshold version is easier than compromising the integrity of a conventional non-threshold version; if compromising the confidentiality in the conventional implementation is easier than compromising the confidentiality of **all** n ($= 1 + f_C$) nodes in the threshold version (when $f_C = n - 1$). In some attack/compromise models it may be possible to quantify the likelihood of $f + 1$ nodes being compromised, e.g., dependent on an attack intensity and rejuvenation pattern [BB12]. In particular, one may find that under certain models the threshold property induces less reliability or availability if not properly provisioned with rejuvenation mechanisms. If, for example, nodes are of similar type, such as several hardware security modules (HSMs) or several virtual machines (VMs) in different computers and have *diversity* at certain levels (OS, vendor, etc.), and if a constant rate probability of compromise is plausible for certain attack vectors, then it is possible to analyze the impact of reactive and proactive rejuvenation.

Consider the mentioned case with threshold $f_I = 0$ for integrity. In a context where integrity is as important as confidentiality, can the above mentioned scheme still be appropriate? Yes, since the difficulty of compromising each property may vary with the conceived type of attack on the implementation. For example: compromising confidentiality may be possible by *passively* exploiting side-channel leakage from a set of nodes; compromising integrity may require actively intruding a node to (maliciously) change an internal state (e.g., an incorrect share). Particularly, a security property P_1 having a compromise threshold value f_1 lower than the threshold f_2 of another property P_2 does not imply that P_1 is easier to break than P_2. Thus, there may be scenarios justifying a threshold scheme with a high threshold for some properties, even if with a low threshold (including $f = 0$) for others. Properties with associated threshold 0 may possibly also be distinctively protected per node, e.g., based on standard non-threshold techniques. Also, as already mentioned with an example for integrity, some properties with a low threshold in a threshold scheme module may be considered in an adjusted way at the application layer, if the application can handle the compromise of a property (e.g., integrity) in the threshold scheme. (Still, the compromise of some properties, such as confidentiality of a key, may often be undetectable).

4.1.2   A word of caution: pitfalls of decoupling security properties

A simplistic decoupling of security properties may lead to pitfalls. An enumeration of separate security properties (e.g., privacy of input and correctness of output) may sometimes fail to capture relevant dependencies or other independent properties. A typical example in cryptography research is related to commitment schemes, useful for auction applications as follows: first, each agent independently commits to a chosen bid, in a way that *hides* its value but *binds* the agent to the value; then all agents reveal their bids in a verifiable way, and the one with the highest bid wins. An over-simplistic analysis of the application could determine that the commitment would only need to ensure *hiding* and *binding* properties — respectively mappable to confidentiality and integrity properties. However, this would fail to capture a needed property of *non-malleability* [DDN03]: upon seeing a commitment from someone else, an agent should not be able to produce a new commitment that commits to a value related to the originally committed value, and which the agent is able to open upon seeing the opening of the original commitment. There are hiding-and-binding commitments that are simultaneously malleable [Ped92], which would be ill-suited to the mentioned application.

In contrast to the mentioned pitfall, there are formal methods for defining and proving security. For example, the ideal-real simulation paradigm [Can01] provides an abstraction that captures the intended application in an ideal world. Starting with such modeling, one can then deduce diverse properties, such as confidentiality, integrity and availability, among others (e.g. non-repudiation, or plausible deniability). If some intended property is not present, then the specified ideal world is not capturing the intended functionality, and perhaps a different ideal version should be specified. This formal approach may offer useful properties, such as composability, allowing upper layer protocols to be analyzed by replacing the threshold protocol by a corresponding ideal functionality.

The above mentioned considerations are also pertinent when changing from a conventional scheme to a threshold scheme. The threshold augmentation may require adjusting an ideal functionality and/or adding definitions and security properties. For example, the communication between components of the threshold scheme may be subject to attacks/compromises that affect security in a way that is not possible in the non-threshold version (where the notion of communication between components is not even applicable). As another example, a security property defined with the help of a "game" (a game-based definition), where an adversary has some access to an "oracle" (e.g., an encryption oracle), may have to update the game definition (including the definition of a success) to account for the possibility of several components being controlled by the adversary.

4.1.3   Specific attacks

As just conveyed, there is a phase of security assessment that justifies care about pitfalls of basing the analysis on a limited number of security properties. In that regard, we assume as baseline that a conventional implementation already implicitly satisfies the security requisites of an intended context. For example, if we discuss a block-cipher or a signature algorithm, then we assume we are talking of corresponding algorithms already suitable under some formal model. In other words, the reference conventional system would be secure if its implementation was not subject to compromise in the real world. It is then that we position our perspective about threshold schemes in a setting that considers specific attack vectors in the real world. These attacks, exploiting differences between conventional implementations and their idealized versions, may sometimes be focused on specific security properties, e.g., confidentiality of a key. For possible relations between threshold parameters (e.g., f and n), other features (see Sec. 5), and the assumed difficulty to perform exploits (e.g., per node), we consider how threshold approaches can affect (e.g., improve) security properties of interest. This may include asking how difficult it is to compromise more than f parties, and/or to extract meaningful information from leakage collected from a threshold scheme. To be clear, this is not incompatible with threshold schemes being themselves provably secure within formal models of security, e.g., within the ideal/real simulation paradigm. Our focus is in asking how and which threshold schemes may improve security in the real world.

We have been focusing on attacks against the confidentiality of a key, but attacks can have other goals. An attack focused on breaking availability can try to accomplish a *denial of service* of some cryptographic operation. The consequences can be catastrophic if the operation is part of a time-sensitive critical mission. Threshold schemes also provide tradeoffs for availability. If nodes can only fail by crash, better availability can typically be obtained by increasing the overall number of nodes n, while keeping k constant. However, if nodes can become malicious, then availability (of correct operations, i.e., with integrity) requires handling faulty nodes. The cost (in n) for handling faulty nodes may vary significantly based on the ability vs. inability to detect and replace faulty nodes and may impose restrictions on f and k.

4.1.4　Proofs of Security

Proofs of security are essential in state-of-the-art cryptography. Their importance in supporting proposals of cryptographic schemes is recognized in the "NIST Cryptographic Standards and Guidelines Development Process" document, published by the Cryptographic Technology Group in 2016 [Gro16]. These proofs can serve as a guide to follow a logical path to assess the security of a threshold scheme, being useful to identify assumptions and attack models on which to base security assertions. This can, for example, be helpful to compare security of a threshold scheme vs. the security of a corresponding conventional (non-threshold) scheme. Proofs are characterized by different attributes, e.g.: contextualized to adversary types (e.g., see Sec. 4.2), security parameters (e.g., computational and/or statistical) and other characteristics of a system model (e.g., see Sec. 4.3); proving an enumeration of security properties vs. proving that a scheme (protocol) emulates an ideal functionality; proving security in a standalone setting vs. establishing security under composition with other protocol executions; being thorough in modeling the real world vs. omitting consid-

Table 1. Representative attack types

Type	Representative question
passive vs. active	Does the attack affect the specified protocol flow?
static vs. adaptive	To which extent are the choices of the attacker based on observations of the protocol execution?
communication interfaces vs. side-channels	Is the attack based on information channels not modeled in the protocol specification?
detectable vs. undetectable	Is the system aware of (e.g., reacts to or logs evidence of) attempted attacks and/or successful intrusions?
invasive vs. non-invasive	Does an attack require physical access to and/or does it affect the physical structure of a device?
threshold-related vs. similar between non-threshold and nodes	Is an attack on the threshold scheme a straightforward generalization (e.g., parallel or sequential attack to nodes) of a possible attack to the conventional implementation?

eration of possible real side-channels. Proofs may also vary with the primitive type and research area, e.g., single-device setting (e.g., threshold circuits) vs. general SMPC. Overall, results from state-of-the-art research can provide useful insights on these choices.

4.2 Types of attack

Security goals are considered with respect to an adversary, also known as an "attacker". When evaluating a proposal for threshold scheme implementation, we would like to have a sense of the range of adversarial scenarios that it may be able to withstand. As a baseline to crosscheck security assertions, we consider several attack types, as enumerated in Table 1. This is not intended as a full characterization or rigorous taxonomy, but it helps us recall and differentiate relevant cases when considering threshold schemes.

Passive vs. active. A passive attacker (or a passively corrupted node) does not change the flow of the prescribed protocol execution, but may gain knowledge of the internal state of some participants, as well as read the content transmitted via communication channels. In active attacks, some components may be subject to intrusion and behave arbitrarily differently from the protocol specification; in the later case, the attacker may also interfere with the communication channels, by altering, dropping and/or reordering messages.

Static vs. adaptive. In static attacks, the attack pattern, e.g., the choice of which components to try to compromise, does not depend on observations of the protocol execution. In adaptive attacks, the attacker can adapt the adversarial actions based on an observation of the protocol flow. For example, a node may be targeted for intrusion upon being elected to a role of *leader* in a phase of the protocol.

Communication interfaces vs. side-channels.   Some attacks can be perpetrated via regular communication channels, though possibly using specially crafted messages. For example, a corrupted client may send an invalid message to a node of a threshold scheme in order to exploit a buffer-overflow vulnerability. Other attacks can be based on *side-channels*, as mentioned in Sec. 3.2, taking advantage of an information flow outside the scope of the explicitly designated communication interface of the system.

Detectable vs. undetectable.   Attacks may be detectable (and detected or undetected) or undetectable. The latter may happen due to adversaries that are able to bypass possible attack-detection mechanisms. They may also result from blatant attacks, if the attacked system is nonetheless unprepared for detection. When a system does not detect being under attack or having been compromised, it is unable to initiate reactive measures of attack mitigation. It may nonetheless have proactive measures in place, triggered at regular intervals of time, e.g., replacing components that might or might not meanwhile have been compromised. The prospect of attack detectability may also act as a deterrent against malicious behavior. From a different angle: a stealth attack may lead to a detectable compromise/intrusion; a detectable attack may lead to an undetected compromise/intrusion.

Invasive vs. non-invasive.   Another attack characterization relates to the needed proximity and interaction between the attacker and the physical boundaries of the attacked system. Non-invasive attacks do not require interaction within the physical boundary of the system [ISO12]. Invasive attacks require the attacker to be in the presence of (e.g., "touching") the physical device or be in its immediate proximity. This includes the case of stripping out some coating layers of a device, to reach an area of a circuit that can then be directly probed. This may also include beaming ultra-violet light into particular zones of a circuit (which requires close proximity), to change an internal state (e.g., a lock bit [AK96]) and thereby inducing a change of behavior.

Conventional vs. threshold-related.   While threshold schemes may be designed to mitigate the effectiveness of some attacks on conventional applications, the actual implementation of a threshold design may be the cause of new inherent vulnerabilities. For example, an attack may be able to exploit some vulnerability in the communication network that intermediates several nodes, where such a network would not even exist in a conventional implementation. We characterize an attack as threshold-related if the attack vector is inherently allowed by the threshold design. Complementary, there are conventional attacks that can be considered similarly with respect to each component of a threshold scheme. In the latter case, it is still relevant to consider, for example, if an attacker is able to choose whether to attack the nodes/platform in parallel or sequentially.

Tolerance to compromise can be useful even in scenarios of non-intentional adversaries. For example, some systems may be constrained to satisfy auditability requirements that warrant taking down components for audit. If a service is supported on a multi-party threshold scheme with tolerance to compromise, then the audit of components can be done without affecting the overall availability.

4.3   System model

The goal of this subsection is to convey possible nuances of system models, in order to encourage a reflection of different consequences they may induce. Several characterizing features of system model for threshold schemes are further discussed in Sec. 5.

4.3.1   Interactions

For a security assessment, it is relevant to consider the interaction between the threshold system and its environment. A threshold system, e.g., a module composed of n nodes, usually interacts with its clients/operators, through a medium of communication. The system may also include other interfaces through which a (possibly stealthy) adversary may obtain information and/or actively interact with components of the system. Thus, attack vectors are not limited just to actual intrusion/compromise of nodes, but also to adversarial effects on the environment. For example: corrupted clients may behave maliciously to try to induce a denial of service for other clients; an adversary controlling part of the network might be able to induce a state of inconsistency across different nodes, even if no node in particular can be said to be compromised. We are interested in security properties involving both the threshold entity and the complementary environment.

Besides the n nodes and users/clients, there may also exist special auxiliary components with the task of relaying, proxying and/or aggregating messages. Such components, which we may call *brokers*, can conceivably be outside of the threshold compromise model (i.e., not accounted in n). Particularly, it may be justifiably assumed that a broker does not fail within the attack model considered for the other components. For example, a broker may be a simple stateless web-redirector, independent of the cryptographic computation needed by the threshold components. Conversely, the n nodes accounted for the threshold may be instantiated in a platform more susceptible to certain attacks.

A broker can be used to modularize some concerns, e.g., replacing or substantiating usual assumptions, such as the existence of authenticated channels. Depending on the communication model, the broker can, for example, broadcast messages from clients to all components. At the inter-node level, the broker can be a router at the center of a star configuration, substantiating an inter-node (logical) clique model. The broker can also act as a mediator between each client and the set of nodes of the threshold scheme, possibly hiding from the client the threshold scheme layer. For example, the broker can produce secret shares of the client's messages and then only send these shares to the nodes; in the reverse direction, it can check consistency, and possibly perform error correction, and aggregate replies from a threshold number of nodes, to then just send a consolidated reply to the client. Depending on the protocol, the threshold nature can be hidden or not from the client. Even in the broker case, the threshold nature of the scheme may, as a feature, be intentionally revealed to the client. For example, the client may receive a multi-signature enabling non-repudiation of the participation of a number of nodes in the production of a response.

The security of a cryptographic service also depends on the communication model. Conceivably, an attacker may be able to eavesdrop, delay, drop, corrupt and/or forge messages in a number of communication channels. A protocol secure in the case of synchronous, fail-safe (messages always delivered) and authenticated channels may become insecure if the channel conditions change. Thus, the characterization of the communication model is essential to contextualize security claims about a threshold scheme. Main characterizing parameters include the existence or lack of synchrony, authentication and encryption. Also, the presence of certain trusted components (or trusted setups) may significantly affect the capabilities of the system. For example, the existence of trusted clocks may sometimes be sufficient to counteract certain difficulties imposed by asynchronous communication channels. It is specifically pertinent to justify when the communication medium should be protected with some mechanism, such as transport layer security (TLS), Internet protocol security (IPSec) or others.

4.3.2 Identity trust

It is easy to leave implicit certain assumptions about the identities of nodes involved in a threshold scheme, but different settings lead to different results. Who decides and enforces who the participants (nodes) of a multi-party threshold scheme are? Is the identity of each party verifiable by other parties? Is the set of parties constant, does it change in a well-defined manner, or is it arbitrarily open to new membership?

In an easy scenario, no new nodes join after the onset of a threshold scheme, and their identities remain valid throughout their lifetimes. A *dealer* knowing a secret can define the setup configuration, deploying nodes, establishing their identities and possibly even the inter-node communication channels. The dealer then distributes shares of the secret and delegates the threshold execution of some cryptographic primitive.

A threshold scheme may also be implemented in a setting where the nodes have identities tied to public keys within a public-key infrastructure (PKI). The PKI can then support secure authentication and communication (e.g., with confidentiality and integrity of content and origin) between any pair of nodes. (This assurance assumes that the attacker may control the delivery of messages between nodes but cannot prevent nodes from accessing the root certification authority.) With PKI-based signatures, a threshold scheme can be designed to enable external users to verify that results were indeed obtained upon a threshold interaction.

In a different setting, the initial state of parties might be defined by a joint protocol, e.g., a distributed key generation [Ped92]. The joint computation may yield to every node a share of a new secret, possibly along with authentication credentials. This can conceivably be used by a certification authority (CA) to generate a new signing key, without ever having it available (for leakage) in any localized point. In such case, there is no use for a trusted dealer of shared secrets, although the nodes may still have been deployed by the same entity.

Some systems may need or benefit from being dynamic with respect to the number of participants in a protocol. This may involve allowing different parties to dynamically enter the protocol, thereby making the threshold parameters f and n variable (perhaps while maintaining a fixed f/n ratio). What if there is no verifiability criterion for the legitimacy of a new intended guest participant? In a Sybil attack [Dou02] a single entity can forge multiple entities perceived as valid, thereby easily breaking any fixed threshold ratio f/n (< 1) of compromisable components. Some mitigation measures may involve enforcing a cost of participation per party, e.g., performing some cryptographic puzzle [JB99].

In more controlled settings, there may be a requirement that new parties be able to prove belonging to an allowed group. This may be based on a PKI certificate signed by an authority. Some scenarios can justify having a dynamic number of parties in an actual threshold scheme for cryptographic primitives. This may happen, for example, in the case of an implementation with a system of intrusion detection and proactive and reactive refreshing of nodes. There may be times when the system must refresh some nodes, and due to a high rate of reactive refreshing it may temporarily have no additional nodes to join.

4.3.3   Trust between clients and threshold scheme

We have emphasized the use of threshold schemes as a way to enhance the protection of secret keys. But when the threshold system is then used to, say, encrypt or sign messages at the request of a client, is there a concern about confidentiality of the plaintext? An intention to ensure confidentiality of the plaintext may dictate restrictions on the type of threshold scheme and system model. If the plaintext is to remain secret, then the client cannot simply send the plaintext in clear to one or several of the nodes. Alternatively, it may for example: (i) send it through a trusted proxy that creates and sends a corresponding plaintext share to each node; or (ii) it may communicate directly a share to each node; or (iii) it may encrypt shares for each node but send them through a single primary node. Each example may be supported by a nuanced system model, e.g., respectively (i) the existence of a special trusted component; (ii) a communication model where each client can directly communicate with each node; (iii) a PKI (or shared symmetric keys) enabling encrypted communication with each node.

We can also consider the assurances that a client would like to receive from a threshold scheme operation. We already referred to the possibility of a client receiving independent signatures (or multi-signatures) from the nodes. Going further, we can also think of clients wanting to obtain assurance of correct behavior by the nodes. This can be achieved, for example, with the support of publicly verifiable secret sharing (PVSS) schemes [Sta96, Sch99].

Another matter related to the relation between users and threshold system is authentication and authorization of users. Cryptographic modules often have to support an access control mechanism to determine from which users to accept which requests for cryptographic operations. Access control can itself be implemented using a threshold approach.

4.3.4 Distributed agreement/consensus

To explain the importance of defining a system model, we use the distributed agreement/consensus problem — fundamental in the area of distributed systems — to illustrate how varying models can lead to a wide variability of results. This is a relevant problem for threshold schemes, namely for certain multi-party implementation settings. The goal of *consensus* is to ensure that all good parties within a group of n parties agree on a value proposed by one of the good parties, even if up to f-out-of-n parties are compromised. For example, this may be necessary for letting a multi-party system decide which cryptographic operations to perform in which order, when the system receives concurrent requests, possibly maliciously delivered, from multiple users.

Results relating n and f within this setting include many impossibilities [Lyn89], with myriad nuances depending on communication and failure models. In one extreme, the problem is unsolvable deterministically in a completely asynchronous setting [FLP85], even with (non-transferable) authentication and a single crash-stop process (which can only fail by crashing). Yet, realistic subtle nuances of the system model circumvent the impossibility.

For example, the problem is solvable even with Byzantine faults if the processes have access to randomness [Ben83, Rab83] or synchronous communication [PSL80, LSP82, DDS87]. In those settings the number of good components must be larger than two-thirds of the total, i.e., $k \geq (2n+1)/3$, or equivalently $n \geq 3f+1$. Provided the appropriate timing assumptions, if nodes only fail by crash then a non-crashed simple-majority is sufficient, i.e., $k \geq f+1$, or equivalently $n \geq 2f+1$ [Lam06]. In another extreme, consensus is solvable even with a single good party if a suitable trusted setup can be instantiated to enable transferable message authentication. This is the case when a PKI setup enables cryptographic signatures [PSL80], or in some other setups (e.g., reliable broadcast and secret channels in a precomputation phase [PW92]).

The discussion above motivates reflecting also on the property of brittleness [Vas15]. This expresses a degree of susceptibility to a breakdown of the security properties (e.g., exfiltration of a key) of a particular algorithm due to errors in the configuration and/or input parameters. In other words, one is concerned with the fragility of a system with respect to changes in the system model or expected setup. Even if a system has all desired properties under a well-defined model, it may be unsuitable for real deployment if it fails catastrophically under reasonable variations of the environment. One would typically prefer instead some kind of graceful degradation. Also related and pertinent is the consideration of how protocols behave differently under different types of attack. Some protocols can be characterized by two (or more) ordered thresholds (e.g, $f_1 < f_2$), meaning that desired security properties hold while the first threshold is not surpassed, but the security failure is not catastrophic while the second threshold is not met [FHHW03]. The thresholds can also depend on the type of attackers, and different nodes can be subject to different types of compromise.

5   Characterizing features

We now provide a high-level structured review of characterizing features of threshold schemes, to facilitate the discussion towards criteria for evaluation of concrete proposals. We intend to motivate a characterization that helps clarify security tradeoffs when reflecting on diverse adversarial models. Put differently, we find that the upfront clarification of certain high-level features is important for discussing the standardization and validation of threshold cryptographic schemes. Table 2 shows examples of possible representations and attributes of characterizing features — it does not intend to be exhaustive.

5.1   Threshold values

5.1.1   A threshold

From within a total number n of components, a "threshold" can be expressed in two ways: a minimum required number k of *good* (i.e., non-compromised) components; or a maximum allowed number f of *bad* (i.e., compromised) components. Correspondingly, the dual threshold notation — f vs. k — enables us to pinpoint each perspective, which can be useful. For example: in some cases, a design goal is directly set as the ability to withstand the compromise of up to a threshold number f of components; in other cases, design constraints such as cost may directly limit the total number n of components, which in turn may impose a threshold number k of good components, depending on the protocol and adversarial model.

As already discussed in Sec. 4.1.1, these thresholds (of *good* and *bad* number of components) make sense when contextualized (sometimes implicitly) to some security property. For example, when referring to a k-out-of-n secret sharing scheme the k refers to availability (minimum number of components necessary to recover a secret), whereas the compromise threshold f for confidentiality of the secret (maximum number of components that together cannot recover the secret) is in that case equal to $k - 1$. The meanings of *good* and *bad* and the corresponding thresholds can vary across different security properties. The threshold

Table 2. Characterizing features of threshold schemes

Feature	Representation	Examples
Threshold type	Threshold numbers of bad (f) and good (k) nodes	max $f = 0, ...\ (n-1)/3, (n-1)/2, n-1$ or min $k = n, ...\ 2f+1, f+1, 1$
Threshold type	Variation with security property and attack vector	$(k_{\text{Secrecy}}, k_{\text{Integrity}}) = (1, n),$ $((n-1)/2, (n-1)/2), ..., (n, 1)$
Threshold type	Compromise across nodes	common; independent; sequential
Communication interfaces	Client $\leftrightarrow$ crypto module	broadcast; primary node; secret-sharing
Communication interfaces	Inter-node structure	star; clique
Communication interfaces	Channel protection	TLS; IPSec; dedicated physical connections; trusted paths [NIS01]; application-level encryption
Target executing platforms	Multiple parties vs. single device	multiple interacting computers; multi-chip in single device; threshold circuit design
Target executing platforms	Software vs. hardware	VMs as components; HSM; crypto accelerators; crypto libraries; trusted computing environments
Target executing platforms	Auxiliary components	global clock; proxy; combiner; random number generator (RNG)
Setup and maintenance	Bootstrap support	dealer; SMPC
Setup and maintenance	Rejuvenation modes	reactive vs. proactive; parallel vs. sequential
Setup and maintenance	Diversity generation	offline pre-computation vs. on-the-fly; unbounded vs. limited set
Setup and maintenance	Diversity levels	operating system; CA; access control; location; vendor; processor architecture; randomization

symbols k and f can be indexed by the corresponding security property (e.g., f_C vs. f_I vs. f_A, respectively for confidentiality, integrity and availability), but we omit indices when the context is clear.

5.1.2   Relating n vs. f and k

When analyzing proposals for concrete threshold schemes, we intend that the system model be sufficiently characterized to enable determining allowed relations between n vs. f and k. Furthermore, it is important to understand how these thresholds can have an extreme variation across security properties.

As one example, a n-out-of-n secret-sharing scheme has an optimal threshold for confidentiality ($f_C = n - 1$, i.e., $k_C = 1$) and at the same time a pessimal threshold for integrity ($f_I = 0$, i.e., $k_I = n$) and availability ($f_A = 0$, i.e., $k_A = n$).

For another example, consider a threshold randomness-generator, intended to output uniformly random bit-strings, periodically or upon request. In a particular specification, the output randomness can be defined as the XOR of bit-string contributions from several generators of randomness (the components of the threshold scheme). The output is then uniformly random if at least one (good) contribution is a uniformly random bit-string that is independent of the other contributions. Note that the guarantees for independence are important but out of scope for this report. Thus, this scheme has an optimal integrity threshold, i.e., $(k_I, f_I) = (1, n-1)$, with respect to guaranteeing the uniformly random property of a produced output. However, if an output generation requires the participation of all components, then the scheme also has the worst threshold for availability, i.e., $(k_A, f_A) = (n, 0)$, since a single bad party can boycott the output.

In comparison, the two examples have the same availability thresholds ($f_A = 0$), but different integrity thresholds: pessimal ($f_I = 0$) in the first example and optimal $f_I = n-1$) in the second example. Furthermore, confidentiality is a relevant property with optimal threshold ($f_A = n-1$) in the first example, whereas it is not even applicable in the second example.

5.1.3   Different thresholds for the same scheme

We gave examples for how the same threshold scheme may be characterized by different thresholds for different security properties. Going further, the thresholds may vary even for a fixed qualitative property (e.g., confidentiality, or integrity, or availability). Typically, an active/malicious/byzantine adversary induces a lower fault-tolerance threshold (i.e., lower tolerance to compromise), when compared to a passive and/or crash-only adversary. The same is true for system model assumptions, such as asynchrony vs. synchrony of communication channels, and the absence vs. existence of a trusted setup such as a public-key infrastructure. The distributed consensus problem in Sec. 4.3.4 shows how a threshold can vary widely depending on the setting.

The determination of relevant threshold values can also depend on the primitives used and the application context, e.g., how the actual threshold scheme is used in connection with other entities. In some applications, a client can check the validity of signatures obtained upon request to a threshold signature module. If a detection of an incorrect signature allows a proper reaction, then a threshold signature scheme can be useful even if its integrity does not tolerate compromised components (i.e., if $f = 0$). One could then argue that the application itself allows a different threshold for integrity. Similar verifiability with respect to decryption, or symmetric-key encryption, may be more difficult/costlier, though not impossible. In fact, certain threshold schemes can be directly built with a property (often called robustness) that prevents integrity violations when up to a threshold number of parties misbehave. For example, this can be based on verifiable secret sharing schemes, which allow verification of correct use of shares. It can also be based on zero-knowledge proofs of correct behavior.

In the simplest form, a threshold f is a number that defines a simple partition of subsets, distinguishing the set of subsets with more than f nodes from the remaining subsets. It is worth noticing that the concept can extend to more general partitions [ISN89, HM00].

5.1.4 Representative questions about threshold values

1. For each desired security property, what are the threshold values (maximum f and/or minimum k), as a function of the total number n of components?

2. What envisioned application contexts justify a high threshold for some properties at the cost of a low threshold for other properties (or of other mitigation measures)?

3. How do threshold values vary with respect to conceivable variations of the system model (e.g., synchrony vs. asynchrony, passive vs. active adversaries)?

5.2 Communication interfaces

The augmentation from a conventional cryptographic implementation to a threshold scheme impacts the communication model. Conceivably, a client can now communicate with more than one component (hereafter "node"), and the nodes can communicate between themselves. In Sec. 4.3.1 we already described several nuances of system model, including synchrony vs. asynchrony, and the possible existence of a broker. We now briefly describe three nuances of communication structures related to clients and nodes.

5.2.1 Client to/from primary node

The client may communicate with the threshold scheme via a single contact component. When such component is one of the n nodes of the threshold scheme, we can call it a primary node for communication. It relays to all other nodes the communication from the client (e.g., a plaintext), and inversely the result (e.g., a signature). For example, it aggregates intermediate results produced by other components, to then send a single consolidated reply to the client. In such a setting the system might, for example with respect to availability, not be able to tolerate the failure of the primary node (if this role does not change across nodes). But other threshold properties, e.g., confidentiality sustained on a secret sharing scheme across all nodes, may remain independent of the use or not of a primary.

5.2.2 From client to all nodes

If the client is aware of the threshold scheme, it may be able to replicate a request across all components. A possible advantage is ensuring that all correct components receive the same request. Correspondingly, the client may also receive replies from all (or a threshold number of) components and only then decide on a final result. In a different implementation model, the client can perform secret-sharing on the input and then communicate one share per component. This can be used to support confidentiality of the input, e.g., a plaintext to encrypt or sign. At the very least, this prevents components from applying corruptions dependent on the plaintext value. In the reverse direction, the client can reconstruct (possibly with error-correction) an output from a set of replied shares.

5.2.3   Inter-node communication

In typical threshold schemes, the components have to directly communicate between themselves. (An exception is when the client is the sole intermediary between nodes). The inter-node network structure influences the efficiency and security of communication. In a star configuration, a primary node intermediates all communication. In a clique configuration (i.e., a complete graph), all nodes are able to directly contact any other node. For efficiency reasons, a star configuration may be used for most communication and a clique configuration be available for secondary communications. A dynamic selection of the primary node (also known as leader) may enable overcoming cases of it being compromised [CL02].

5.2.4   Representative questions about communication interfaces

1. Are clients aware of the threshold nature of the implementation?

2. How is the initial request from a client propagated through the set of nodes?

3. How can the inter-node communication be compromised?

4. How does the client obtain a consolidated reply based on a set of partial results produced by a set of nodes?

5. How is the logical/physical "boundary" [NIS18c] of the system affected by the existing communication channels?

5.3   Target computing platforms

To some extent, the implementation platform can be abstracted from some functional properties of a threshold scheme. Yet, there are distinctive platform-related aspects relevant for security assessment and validation. We elaborate here on three main instances: single-device vs. multi-party; software vs. hardware; and auxiliary components. These aspects can affect other features and are relevant for the development of validation profiles.

5.3.1   Software vs. hardware

Cryptography is implemented on a variety of computing platforms. In the early days of the modern technological revolution in computing and communications, cryptographic algorithms were implemented predominantly in hardware. Examples of such embodiments are the secure phone lines between federal offices in the 1970s. Hardware implementations provide a level of isolation of the sensitive cryptographic keys and their utilization in processing information, along with storage and management of keys and other sensitive parameters.

It is natural to think of the physical boundary of a dedicated circuit board, a dedicated chip, a smart card, or USB key. Thus, one can relate that physical boundary to the ideal black box boundary introduced in Sec. 4 and formulate a set of security assertions. This in fact is the foundation for FIPS 140-2 [NIS01], which was initially developed for hardware cryptographic implementations. This standard contains specific security requirements on the physical boundary of hardware modules, namely in Ref. [NIS01, Section 4], which are concerned with ensuring the attacker cannot probe the circuitry and extract the keys.

As the adoption of cryptography extended into e-commerce over the Internet, software implementations of cryptography emerged and over the years became a widely used embodiment for cryptographic primitives. Software cryptographic implementations on a general purpose computer (GPC) are just like any other software component that runs within the control of an operating system (OS). GPCs are much more porous (see Sec. 1) and tend to provide fewer assurances with respect to the isolation of cryptographic keys and other security-sensitive parameters from unauthorized access by other applications running on the same GPC/OS platform, or remotely through the network interfaces of the platform. Correspondingly, these software modules are subject only to a subset of the security requirements described in Ref. [NIS01] and are limited to a lower level of security assurances they can claim to deliver.

Given this historical context, the distinction of hardware vs. software in FIPS 140-2 comes from the difference in isolation that the approaches provide, and is not directly related to the manner in which the computation is performed. Note, for example, that an HSM might actually contain an embedded microcontroller that performs the cryptographic computation in *software*. Also, some hardware platforms such as a Field-Programmable Gate Arrays (FPGAs) can be "reprogrammed," a property that was historically reserved for software implementations. For the sake of readability, we will assume a more "traditional" separation between hardware and software, focusing primarily on the isolation properties, rather than on different types of computing platforms.

The hybrid approach to cryptographic implementations aims to benefit from the flexibility in software and the isolation and/or acceleration in hardware. Here a portion of the implementation is in software executing on a GPC/OS platform and another portion is executing on a dedicated HSM attached to the same GPC. Examples of such modules are the Trusted Platform Module (TPM) [Mor11], or the cryptographic extensions of standard Central Processing Unit (CPU) instruction sets, such as the Software Guard Extensions (SGX) instruction on Intel platforms [Int18], and the TrustZone technology on Advanced RISC Machine (ARM) processors [ARM18]. These modules can also be used as secure sub-components within a hybrid fault model. The "secure" components have a more restricted mode of compromise (e.g., only by crash), thereby enabling better thresholds for byzantine fault tolerance of a distributed system composed also of larger and less secure components [VCB⁺13, BDK17].

In some cases, a specific cryptographic primitive is implemented partially in software and partially in hardware. For example, an RSA signature algorithm may be implemented in such a way that the modulo exponentiation is executed in hardware but the required padding of the data is implemented in software. In other cases, an entire suite of fully implemented cryptographic primitives is implemented in an HSM and used by a software component through application programming interfaces (API).

The hybrid approach offers important security advantages for implementing crypto- graphic primitives and key management in isolation, as well as performance improve- ments. For example, a hybrid implementation could potentially mitigate cold-boot at- tacks [HSH⁺09], which allows keys to be recovered in seconds or even minutes after it has been removed from the device. Cold-boot attacks typically assume that the keys are stored in the virtual memory of the operating system, and might therefore be moved into DRAM. An HSM could mitigate this attack by ensuring that keys never leave the HSM.

Another reason to delegate the execution of cryptographic primitives to dedicated hardware is for performance improvement. An example of this is the AES extension on Intel [Gue09] and Advanced Micro Devices (AMD) CPUs [AMD12]. HSMs offer similar acceleration benefits.

5.3.2 Single device vs. multi-party

When a threshold scheme is developed to enable tolerance to the compromise of several components, it is intuitive to think of a set of interacting parties (also known as nodes or devices). For example, a *multi-party* threshold setting can be composed of n computers communicating over the Internet, or n hardware security modules (HSMs) connected via a private network, or n virtual machines (VMs) running within the same hardware machine. The connectivity may be dynamic, with the components being possibly replaceable for testing, updating and patching. In a multi-party computation, the nodes may be separated by a network, possibly asynchronous, inherently outside of the control of the threshold scheme. For testing and validation, the tester/validator might not be able to simulate a realistic communication medium between multiple parties.

In contrast to the alluded multi-party systems, we also consider "single device" settings. Main distinctive aspects include, typically, a somewhat rigid configuration of components and a well-defined physical boundary. If the device is a hardware circuit, then in most cases the connections between inner wires and gates are fixed throughout the life of the device. However, there are technologies that actually allow even those components to be adapted across the lifetime of the device, e.g. FPGA. Communication synchrony between components is often expected and achieved. Threshold schemes are applicable to the single-device setting by means of an inner threshold design. There, the inputs and outputs of a threshold circuit become encodings (e.g, sets of secret shares) of the inputs and outputs of the conventional (non-threshold) circuit. For confidentiality, the threshold property may be that no isolated subset of up to f wires in the threshold circuit contains information about any bit that would be flowing in the original circuit. A main application of this design is providing increased resistance against certain side-channel attacks [NRR06].

There is flexibility in distinguishing, and identifying similarities, between multi-party and single-device scenarios. For example, we could imagine the physical components within a device with a threshold design to be multiple "parties". Conversely, a single-device may indeed not have any redundancy of hardware components, and yet a threshold scheme be applied by means of repeated executions of an algorithm. The value of distinguishing the platforms is in facilitating a categorization of aspects that may justify different standardization and/or validation profiles. For example, in a multi-party setting it may be easier to isolate, replace and test corruption of a singular component, for the purpose of validating properties of an implementation. In some single-device cases, it may be infeasible to achieve complete separation of components to test their individual correctness.

5.3.3 Auxiliary components

Threshold schemes may require essential components beyond those accounted in n. To use a distinctive term, we call them *auxiliary* components. These may include, for example, a trusted global clock, a proxy, a common random (or pseudo-random) bit generator, a combiner of information from components. Having a threshold-scheme characterization that acknowledges these components enables a better system model for security assessment. For example: a trusted (assumed trustworthy) clock may be what enables synchrony in a system model, which in turn can influence the threshold and the protocol; the interaction with a trusted random number generator may be necessary to take advantage of the threshold design of a circuit based on secret-sharing; we have also already given examples of how the auxiliary components may affect the inter-node and the client-node communication interfaces. The auxiliary components may have their own compromise model, and their testing and validation is also needed when testing and validating a threshold system. Yet, it is foreseeable that a great deal of analysis about the auxiliary components can be modularized away from threshold-related arguments.

5.3.4 Representative questions about computing platforms

1. If a proposed threshold scheme is devised for a "single-device" setting, what can go wrong if its components are instead separated and communicate over the Internet?

2. Which parts of the logical boundary of the threshold system do not correspond to a physical boundary, as verified by the system developer or deployer?

3. Is the system simply developed at the software layer, or are there software components tied to particular hardware components?

4. Which auxiliary components support the threshold scheme but have a failure model different from the one applied to the threshold nodes?

5.4 Setup and maintenance

In some settings a threshold scheme can be implemented from scratch as an alternative to a construction with a single point of failure. In other cases the starting point is exactly an existing single-point-of-failure entity, which is intended to be redesigned as a threshold system. To compare the effects from the change, we should consider how the system is bootstrapped, including "who" deploys the nodes, and their initial states. Also relevant is the setup of the communication network and continued maintenance of the system, including during detection and/or recovery of compromised components.

5.4.1 Dealer vs. dealer-free setup

In secret sharing, a "dealer" is an entity, possibly outside the failure model of the threshold scheme, that knows a secret and "deals" shares of it to the nodes of the threshold scheme. In a possible scenario, a key holder in a safe environment deals shares of a long-term signature key to nodes that operate in a threshold manner in a less-secure environment. The role of a dealer is not necessarily limited to applications related to secret keys. As a practical example, a setup phase can also consist of a trusted party generating and secret sharing so-called "Beaver-triplets" — triplets of field elements (possibly bits) where the third is the product of the first two. The pre-processing of these triplets enables a very-efficient execution of certain secure computation protocols [Bea92].

In a setting with a dealer, it is relevant to consider the extent to which the protocol security withstands or breaks in the presence of misbehavior by the dealer [BR07]. Some protocols can be made secure against an untrusted dealer, with respect to integrity, if the protocol enables parties to verify correctness of the distributed parameters. Other protocols may have security hinge on an assumption of a trusted dealer. Depending on the functionality, there may exist tradeoffs between efficiency and the property of supporting the malicious dealer.

5.4.2 Rejuvenation of nodes

It is desirable that compromising f-out-of-n nodes in a good threshold scheme is not easier than compromising 1-out-of-1 in a conventional scheme. But is such property inherently guaranteed if $f > 0$ and if the process of compromising each node is independent? Not necessarily, even if the compromise of a node requires an independent exploitation effort (e.g., time, computation) per node.

If nodes of a threshold system can only transition from an uncompromised to a compromised state, then the system may be less secure under certain attack vectors. This may be due to an increased attack surface, a sufficiently low f/n ratio and a sufficiently high mission time. This is a well-known result in fault tolerance, as may happen in a basic triple-modular-redundancy design [KK07]. One may also consider adversarial scenarios that induce a probability rate of a node under attack becoming compromised [OY91]. To counteract these transitions, it is possible, and in many settings essential, to implement recovery/replacement/rejuvenation of nodes that can bring nodes back to a "healthy" (uncompromised) state. There is a plethora of possible rejuvenation modes, e.g., reactive vs. proactive, parallel vs. sequential, instantaneous vs. delayed, stateless vs. stateful, etc.

If a compromise is detected, then the corresponding node should be reactively replaced by a healthy version, lest the system eventually converges to all nodes being compromised. If the compromises are not detectable but are nonetheless conceivable, then a proactive recovery should take place. In the threshold signature scheme from Sec. 3, the resharing of the secret key constitutes a parallel rejuvenation of nodes. If there is no persistent intrusion, and the number of compromises never exceeds the allowed threshold, then the resharing brings the whole system back to a pristine state, with all nodes healthy.

The rejuvenation feature brings along a whole new set of considerations, possibly affecting security in non-trivial ways. If the nodes need to be stateful (i.e., hold state about the application), then newly inserted nodes need to be consistently updated, which requires specification as a sub-protocol. The rejuvenation of a previously compromised node may need to diversify some component, to prevent re-exploitation of the same vulnerability [KF95]. The diversification operation may have its own requirements, possibly requiring pre-computation vs. being generated on-the-fly by some sampling procedure.

In some protocols a rejuvenation may have to take place in parallel, e.g., such as the already discussed example of updating key shares, with all online parties being rejuvenated simultaneously. In other cases, rejuvenations may occur sequentially, replacing/recovering each node at a time, especially if the process involves a long downtime. Many of the considerations pertinent to the initial setup of a threshold system are also applicable to the rejuvenation context. For example, is there a "dealer" responsible for setting up the full state of a rejuvenated node or should the state be updated by the set of online nodes?

If a threshold scheme is based on electing a primary node, what happens when the primary node is the one in need of replacement? If a scheme allows reactive and proactive rejuvenations, can an attacker take advantage of knowing the schedule/ordering of the proactive rejuvenations? What happens if the regular threshold scheme performs correctly in an asynchronous environment, but the recovery procedure requires synchrony? Not handling asynchrony in recovery procedures may hide subtle problems [SNV07]. If the regular threshold scheme requires only a simple honest majority, but the corresponding rejuvenation mechanism requires a 2/3 honest majority, then the threshold properties are also affected.

5.4.3 Levels of diversity

Intuitively, a main motivation for threshold schemes is to improve security by withstanding the compromise of some nodes.[4] Yet, a standalone characterization of threshold values does not say anything about the difficulty of compromising the threshold number f of nodes. Consider the case of a common vulnerability, i.e., common across all nodes (e.g., a bug in a common operating system). Once the vulnerability is discovered, an adversary might be able to exploit it with negligible cost to compromise all nodes. In this example, this would then be "as easy" as compromising a conventional scheme with the same vulnerability.

Consider an example where all nodes are symmetric with respect to the threshold protocol, i.e., all implement the same functionality. One can then imagine all nodes being implemented in the same manner, say, the same software, possibly containing a common vulnerability. Conversely, each node can also be programmed for the same functionality via different software versions [CA78]. In practice, common vulnerabilities may occur at multiple levels where the set of nodes is homogeneous, e.g., operating system, network protocol, hardware design, physical location, password. Diversity may be implemented across space (i.e., across the components within a threshold protocol) and time (i.e., replacements and executions across time). In the multi-party case, rejuvenation can happen by actually replacing a physical node by a new one. In certain single-device settings, rejuvenation might be limited to refreshing randomness, while the actual hardware structure remains fixed. In a software setting, rejuvenation may correspond to replacing a virtual machine, or changing some randomness used when compiling a software version. At some levels, there may be a small set of variants (e.g., operating systems), whereas others (e.g., passwords) are impossible to replace.

The use of diversity is a longstanding practice of traditional fault-tolerance, but its use for security is more intricate [LS04]. Implementation-wise, multiple levels of *diversity* (among other properties) may be required to reduce the possibility of common vulnerabilities [SZ05] and to substantiate an assumption that compromising more nodes is more difficult than compromising fewer nodes. A fundamental difficulty is that the level of effort used by an attack vector may be unpredictable until the attack takes place.

5.4.4 Representative questions about setup and maintenance

1. Can a threshold scheme be bootstrapped in both dealer and dealer-free manners?

2. What levels of diversity are envisioned to deter common-mode failures?

---

[4] We also bear in mind the possible mapping of threshold properties into side-channel resistance properties.

3. What dependency of compromise exists across nodes, for envisioned attack vectors?

4. Does the sub-protocol for handling rejuvenations interfere with the system availability?

6 Validation of implementations

6.1 The existing CMVP and FIPS 140-2

Governments recognize cryptography's important role in protecting sensitive information from unauthorized disclosure or modification, and tend to select algorithms with well-established theoretical security properties. For example, US and Canadian federal agencies must use NIST-defined cryptographic algorithm standards to protect sensitive data in computer and telecommunications systems [tC96]. They must also use only validated cryptographic implementations, typically referred to as modules.

As we have pointed out, the correct and bug-free implementation of a cryptographic algorithm and the environment in which it executes are also very important for security. To assess security aspects related to real hardware and software implementations, NIST established the Cryptographic Module Validation Program (CMVP) [NIS18c] in 1995 to validate cryptographic modules against the security requirements in Federal Information Processing Standard (FIPS) Publication 140-2 [NIS01]. The CMVP leverages independent third-party testing laboratories to test commercial-off-the-shelf cryptographic modules supplied by industry vendors.

FIPS 140-2 is a standard defined as a system of conformance security assertions. The security assertions in the standard cover a wide range of cryptographic primitives implemented into various types of physical embodiments called cryptographic modules. The security assertions are grouped into sets, one for each security level. FIPS 140-2 defines four security levels for cryptographic modules. Depending on the type of technology used for a particular module, e.g. software or hardware, the standard defines a subset of applicable security assertions that the module must meet for a chosen security level and module-specific functional capabilities. In turn, the cryptographic primitives approved by NIST and adopted in FIPS 140-2 through Annex A for use in cryptographic modules are also specified as sets of conformance security assertions. This allows the CMVP to work with a reasonably constrained and well-defined set of security assertions that can be validated.

The Common Criteria [Com17] follows a contrasting approach, where one is allowed to define a unique set of security assertions for a target component, often referred to as a target of evaluation (TOE). The goal of the Common Criteria certification then is to evaluate the correctness of the specific security assertions claimed by the TOE. The evaluation is typically much less structured than the validation process in FIPS 140-2, takes longer time and requires substantially higher expertise from the evaluators and validators.

6.2 Integration of threshold cryptographic schemes

When we consider standardizing threshold cryptographic schemes for approved NIST cryptographic primitives, we intend to pursue the approach of conformance security assertions, similar to the approach taken for the cryptographic primitives and modules.

FIPS 140-2 already has security requirements for secret sharing applied to cryptographic keys. Section 4.7.4 of the standard defines security requirements for split-knowledge procedures for security levels 3 and 4, stipulating that *"if knowledge of n key components is required to reconstruct the original key, then knowledge of n − 1 components provides no information about the original key, other than the length."* This can for example be satisfied by implementations of the Shamir and Blakley secret sharing schemes mentioned in Sec. 2.2.

The above-mentioned provision in FIPS 140-2 refers only to secret-sharing and by itself does not ensure that keys are never recombined when needed by an algorithm, which is a main subject of threshold schemes for cryptographic primitives. That provision is thus insufficient to accommodate the plethora of threshold considerations that have been pointed out in this report. Generally speaking, the process towards standardization of threshold schemes may involve reconsidering the adequacy of the validation requirements and where necessary devise new or complementary requirements.

As technology progresses and cryptography becomes ubiquitous in the federal information infrastructure, the number and complexity of modules to be validated increases. This makes it increasingly difficult to detect at validation stage all possible defects that might compromise security. This is one more reason to consider the potential of threshold cryptography in avoiding single points of failure in real implementations. However, similarly to conventional cryptography, the security of the threshold cryptographic implementation may also be impacted by defects introduced as a result of human errors or unsafe optimization by the tools used to compile or synthesize the implementation. Thus, it is important to ensure that the algorithms supporting threshold cryptography are theoretically secure, and to verify that they have been implemented correctly. The definition of guidelines would help develop a structured process of formulating and validating security assertions about threshold cryptographic implementations.

One additional challenge is to enable ways to validate those assertions in an automated fashion. NIST is working with the industry to rebuild its cryptographic validation programs and improve the efficiency and effectiveness of cryptographic module testing in order to reduce the time and cost required for testing while providing a high level of assurance for Federal government consumers. As the NIST cryptographic validation programs evolve, the adoption of new cryptographic technology into them should target the future structure and mechanisms for testing and reporting results [NIS18b]. The current project includes an Industry/NIST collaboration website for automated validation of cryptographic algorithms (ACVP) and cryptographic modules [NIS18a, NIS18b].

It is encouraging to note that automated methods for validating protocol implementations have emerged recently (e.g., [CHH⁺17, BBK17, DLFK⁺17]). This experience may be useful to leverage for the protocols involved in threshold cryptographic schemes.

7 Criteria for standardization

Active research over the last few decades has resulted in a substantial body of literature on threshold cryptographic schemes. Usually there are tradeoffs of threshold values for different security properties, potentially depending on the application context and system model. With appropriate caution, threshold cryptography offers a great potential for strengthening the security of cryptographic implementations. But what criteria should one use to ask for and select from a potential pool of candidate threshold cryptographic schemes?

7.1 Representative questions

We intend this document to promote the development of criteria for evaluation of proposals of threshold cryptographic schemes. Here we list representative questions likely to induce a discussion about this:

1. Characterizing features
   (a) Are the *characterizing features* of the threshold scheme fully described?
   (b) On what *executing platforms* can the scheme be implemented?
   (c) What are the node-*rejuvenation* mechanisms (e.g., resharing or replacement)?
   (d) What are the operational costs and properties of *setup and maintenance*?
   (e) How are nearby components assumed separate/independent vs. *interfering*?

2. Applicability of scheme
   (a) How *efficient/performant* are the operations as a function of threshold parameters?
   (b) Is the scheme applicable to *NIST-approved* cryptographic primitives?
   (c) Do *base primitives* (e.g., oblivious transfer) require independent standardization?
   (d) Is the *system model* applicable to known and relevant application contexts?

3. Implementations
   (a) Should the standard take into account *feasibility and interoperability* on different platforms, e.g., hardware or operating systems?
   (b) Should the standard define *common APIs* for client-side functions?
   (c) What degree of automated protocol validation should be targeted for proposed standards?

4. Implementation vs. security
   (a) How is *diversity* of nodes related to known attack vectors?
   (b) What threshold aspects can lead to *new implementation bugs or misconfiguration*?
   (c) What *trusted setup / assumptions* are required (e.g., dealer, special components)?

(d) How *brittle* is the scheme (likely to break under small environmental variations)?

(e) What faults can be detected and reversed, while identifying the culprit node(s)?

5. Security

(a) What threshold properties relate to resistance against *side-channel attacks* and how?

(b) Are there identified *security tradeoffs* across attack types and configurations?

(c) How does the *reliability* compare against that of a conventional implementation?

(d) What features of *graceful degradation* exist against conceivable failures?

(e) Does the security proof ensure composability useful for conceived deployments?

(f) Can real attacks thwart the trusted setup assumed in the proof of security?

(g) To which degree has/have the proof(s) of security been formally verified?

6. Validation

(a) Do the *security assertions* match / fit into the FIPS 140-2 framework?

(b) How *testable* is the scheme (can security assertions be tested and validated)?

(c) Is there a proposed *automated validation* mechanism?

7. Licensing

(a) What are the *intellectual property* implications and the *licensing* conditions?

8. New standards development

Depending on the adopted approach to developing the new standards, there may be submissions of candidate threshold schemes for evaluation. If such an approach is adopted then potential criteria for quality submissions might include the following:

(a) Are *working implementations* available?

(b) Is *interoperability* between two or more different implementations demonstrated?

(c) Are high-level *use-cases/applications* (e.g., signing, decryption, etc.) feasible?

We need to develop an objective criteria set to support a call for and a selection of schemes for standardization. An actual criteria guideline would elaborate further on each of the above questions, or variations thereof, and possibly others. The development of such criteria would benefit from collaborative public feedback from the cryptography research community, as well as from stakeholders in the government and industry.

In addition, there may exist pertinent questions about what and how to standardize. What flexibility of parametrization should a standard allow? Should there be distinct standardization profiles to separately focus on distinct attribute instantiations, e.g., single-device vs. multi-party platform, side-channel attack vs. intrusion per node? Next, we elaborate a bit further on two additional aspects.

7.2 Standardization at what granularity level?

Current industry guidelines for best practices in cybersecurity [Ver18] recommend active patching of vulnerable components. If in a validated multi-party threshold scheme a node is found to have a serious vulnerability, the node may need to be patched. This would not be a problem if the scheme tolerates the full compromise of at least one node, and/or if it can replace it with another type of (validated) component. In that case, the overall system continues to operate smoothly during the patching and revalidation of the vulnerable component. Thus, when considering the standardization of a particular threshold scheme, there may be value in validating implementations with diverse platforms/implementations for the individual nodes. This example suggests a question about the standardization criteria: what levels of granularity/modularity should be considered for standardization?

While it may be useful to standardize modular components, such development is not on its own sufficient to achieve good standards for threshold schemes for cryptographic primitives. There are difficulties associated with secure composition of secure components into a protocol (e.g., into a threshold scheme). Composability is indeed a recurring subject in the development of secure multi-party computation protocols. It is thus an open question how one should or should not create standards for combining modular components.

Another consideration on what and how to standardize pertains to the potentially large set of available solutions. On the one hand, SMPC provides general techniques that can use common building blocks to enable thresholdizing any cryptographic primitive. On the other hand, there are also specialized (ad-hoc) solutions with techniques tailored to specific primitives and their applications. How should we handle the two types of solutions in the standardization process, both of which are likely to improve over time? Some benchmarking may be helpful for navigating the pool of possibilities and making objective comparisons between ad-hoc and generic solutions. It is important that this process for characterizing such solutions is conducted in a way that invites and encourages participation from all stakeholders.

7.3 Standardization opportunities

At a basic level, secret-sharing schemes can be used to split a secret key while its use is not required, ensuring that a threshold number $f + 1$ of shares is needed to reconstruct the key. However, this by itself does not enable cryptographic primitives to use the key shares instead of the recombined key. Secret sharing alone might also not enable threshold properties for other purposes, such as preventing a corruption of the intended output. The above limitations can be addressed with threshold cryptography (in the broad sense of encompassing threshold schemes for a secure implementation of cryptographic primitives). For example, the computation may be performed on shares of the key, without the need to ever recombine the original key, and enabling threshold security for other properties, including integrity and availability. *What then should be standardized, within the realm of threshold cryptography?*

Threshold schemes have wide applicability, in the sense that there are general techniques to convert a conventional implementation into a threshold version thereof. One can thus ask: for which conventional cryptographic schemes should one consider standardization of a threshold version? On one hand, there is a clear interest in enabling threshold versions of NIST-approved cryptographic primitives. On the other hand, the consideration of standardization of threshold schemes is in itself an opportunity to review suitability for new standards. In this line, we also wonder how the standardization of threshold schemes might also benefit other ongoing NIST efforts of standardization. For example, could elements from the lightweight [MBTM17] and post-quantum cryptography (PQC) [NIS17] projects at NIST be useful for threshold cryptography? Could the schemes considered by those projects also be looked at in the perspective of possible threshold variants? More research is needed. That is why we do not intend here to show any preference about concrete cases, but simply to raise the point for consideration. We believe that a better clarification may arise from a constructive interaction with the research community and other stakeholders.

8   Conclusions

Conventional cryptographic implementations have a single point of failure when the secret key is stored in one location, or when a localized fault breaks integrity of the output or availability of a cryptographic operation. These failure modes can be mitigated by using threshold schemes for a secure implementation of cryptographic primitives. This includes schemes related to secure multi-party computation and intrusion-tolerant distributed systems. Usually, a threshold property is expressed as an f-out-of-n tolerance to compromise, where the compromise of up to f nodes does not break some security property. For example, when up to f parties possess no information about a secret, security against a wide range of side-channel attacks can be achieved under some reasonable assumptions about the distributions of side-channel information. Furthermore, a threshold scheme may even provide resistance against side-channel attacks that collect information correlated across all nodes (beyond the threshold). This is because, in some models, a threshold design may complicate the exploitation of noisy side-channel information.

Threshold schemes can be efficient. For example, we described how a simple threshold RSA signature scheme based on a n-out-of-n secret-sharing has a complexity that increases only linearly with the number of shares, and whose computation is parallelized across several nodes. In such case, the simplicity of the method is based on a mathematical property (a homomorphism) of the underlying structure of the original scheme. In contrast, schemes for other cryptographic primitives, such as some block ciphers, may require significant computational overhead compared to their conventional counterparts. Still, even in those cases the threshold schemes may be practical and justifiable, depending on the intended security assurances and the application context.

The discussion in the preceding sections highlighted nuanced security assertions that can be obtained about threshold cryptographic schemes. The security of such schemes has to be seen through the prism of a security model and possibly considering several system models of implementation. For example, there may be differences between active or passive attacks. To help navigate the landscape of possible schemes, this report enumerated characterizing features and their possible effects. For example: there are potential benefits of rerandomizing the shares of the secret key; properties can be different between multi-device vs. single-device platforms; some security properties are different depending on the communication platform with the environment and between components.

An understanding of a variety of instantiations of characterizing features is necessary for the development of objective criteria for selecting candidates for standardization. For the purpose of standardization and validation, the combination of characterizing features and attack models should be translated into security assertions. The way these can fit into FIPS 140-2 and/or require complementary standardization is a matter for discussion.

We have looked at numerous factors that influence the type of security assessment that can be made about threshold cryptographic schemes. Clearly, threshold cryptography has potential to improve the security of the implementation of cryptographic primitives, provided it is carefully used. There is a clear interest in enabling threshold schemes for already standardized cryptographic primitives. The standardization effort may also constitute an opportunity to consider the case for standardizing new primitives. There are long-standing research results, and the research community is still active in the area.

We intend this report to initiate a discussion on the standardization of threshold cryptographic schemes. We can envision some of the challenges ahead. The most immediate seems to be the development of criteria for and selection of proposals. This document did not put forth such criteria, but motivated the need for one and developed some basis for it.

Once criteria are in place, the selection and standardization of concrete schemes should include an integration with validation methodologies. How then to express security assertions that may fit within FIPS 140-2 or fit well as a complement thereof? What security and implementation profiles should be devised? When tackling these challenges, positive synergies may result from engaging with and incorporating feedback from the research community and other stakeholders.

References

[ABF⁺03] C. Aumüller, P. Bier, W. Fischer, P. Hofreiter, and J.-P. Seifert. *Fault Attacks on RSA with CRT: Concrete Results and Practical Countermeasures*. In B. S. Kaliski, Ç. K. Koç, and C. Paar (eds.), Cryptographic Hardware and Embedded Systems — CHES 2002, vol. 2523 of LNCS, pages 260–275. Springer Berlin Heidelberg, 2003. DOI:10.1007/3-540-36400-5_20.

[AK96] R. Anderson and M. Kuhn. *Tamper Resistance: A Cautionary Note*. Proc. 2nd USENIX Workshop on Electronic Commerce (WOEC'96), 2:1–11, 1996.

[AMD12] AMD Corporation. *AMD has you covered*. https://www.amd.com/Documents/Security_021.pdf, 2012.

[AMGC85] B. Awerbuch, S. Micali, S. Goldwasser, and B. Chor. *Verifiable secret sharing and achieving simultaneity in the presence of faults*. In Proc. 26th Annual Symposium on Foundations of Computer Science, SFCS '85, pages 383–395. IEEE Computer Society, 1985. DOI:10.1109/SFCS.1985.64.

[AMN01] M. Abdalla, S. Miner, and C. Namprempre. *Forward-Secure Threshold Signature Schemes*. In D. Naccache (ed.), Topics in Cryptology — CT-RSA 2001, pages 441–456. Springer Berlin Heidelberg, 2001. DOI:10.1007/3-540-45353-9_32.

[And02] R. Anderson. *Two remarks on public key cryptology*. Technical report, University of Cambridge, Computer Laboratory, 2002.

[ARM18] ARM Corporation. *TrustZone*. https://www.arm.com/products/security-on-arm/trustzone, 2018.

[BB03] D. Brumley and D. Boneh. *Remote Timing Attacks Are Practical*. In Proc. 12th Conference on USENIX Security Symposium — SSYM'03, pages 1–13. USENIX Association, 2003.

[BB12] L. T. A. N. Brandão and A. N. Bessani. *On the reliability and availability of replicated and rejuvenating systems under stealth attacks and intrusions*. Journal of the Brazilian Computer Society, 18(1):61–80, 2012. DOI:10.1007/s13173-012-0062-x.

[BBK17] K. Bhargavan, B. Blanchet, and N. Kobeissi. *Verified Models and Reference Implementations for the TLS 1.3 Standard Candidate*. In 2017 IEEE Symposium on Security and Privacy (SP), pages 483–502. IEEE, may 2017. DOI:10.1109/SP.2017.26.

[BCF00] E. F. Brickell, G. D. Crescenzo, and Y. Frankel. *Sharing Block Ciphers*. In Information Security and Privacy – ACISP 2000, vol. 1841 of LNCS, pages 457–470. Springer Berlin Heidelberg, 2000. DOI:10.1007/10718964_37.

[BDK17] J. Behl, T. Distler, and R. Kapitza. *Hybrids on Steroids: SGX-Based High Performance BFT*. In Proc. 12th European Conference on Computer Systems, EuroSys '17, pages 222–237, New York, NY, USA, 2017. ACM. DOI:10.1145/3064176.3064213.

[BDL97] D. Boneh, R. A. DeMillo, and R. J. Lipton. *On the Importance of Checking Cryptographic Protocols for Faults*. In W. Fumy (ed.), Advances in Cryptology — EUROCRYPT '97, vol. 1233 of LNCS, pages 37–51. Springer Berlin Heidelberg, 1997. DOI:10.1007/3-540-69053-0_4.

[Bea92] D. Beaver. *Efficient Multiparty Protocols Using Circuit Randomization*. In J. Feigenbaum (ed.), Advances in Cryptology — CRYPTO '91, vol. 576 of LNCS, pages 420–432. Springer Berlin Heidelberg, 1992. DOI:10.1007/3-540-46766-1_34.

[Ben83] M. Ben-Or. *Another Advantage of Free Choice (Extended Abstract): Completely Asynchronous Agreement Protocols*. In Proc. 2nd Annual ACM Symposium on Principles of Distributed Computing, PODC '83, pages 27–30. ACM, 1983. DOI:10.1145/800221.806707.

[Ber05] D. J. Bernstein. *Cache-timing attacks on AES*. https://cr.yp.to/antiforgery/cachetiming-20050414.pdf, 2005.

[Ber06] D. J. Bernstein. *Curve25519: New Diffie-Hellman Speed Records*. In M. Yung, Y. Dodis, A. Kiayias, and T. Malkin (eds.), Public Key Cryptography — PKC 2006, vol. 3958 of LNCS, pages 207–228. Springer Berlin Heidelberg, 2006. DOI:10.1007/11745853_14.

[BF97] D. Boneh and M. Franklin. *Efficient generation of shared RSA keys*. In B. S. Kaliski (ed.), Advances in Cryptology — CRYPTO '97, vol. 1294 of LNCS, pages 425–439. Springer Berlin Heidelberg, 1997. DOI:10.1007/BFb0052253.

[BFM88] M. Blum, P. Feldman, and S. Micali. *Non-interactive Zero-knowledge and Its Applications*. In Proc. 20th Annual ACM Symposium on Theory of Computing, STOC '88, pages 103–112. ACM, 1988. DOI:10.1145/62212.62222.

[BGG$^+$14] J. Balasch, B. Gierlichs, V. Grosso, O. Reparaz, and F. Standaert. *On the Cost of Lazy Engineering for Masked Software Implementations*. In Smart Card Research and Advanced Applications — CARDIS, vol. 8968 of LNCS, pages 64–81. Springer Berlin Heidelberg, 2014. DOI:10.1007/978-3-319-16763-3_5.

[BGW88] M. Ben-Or, S. Goldwasser, and A. Wigderson. *Completeness Theorems for Non-cryptographic Fault-tolerant Distributed Computation*. In Proceedings of the Twentieth Annual ACM Symposium on Theory of Computing, STOC '88, pages 1–10, New York, NY, USA, 1988. ACM. DOI:10.1145/62212.62213.

[BH98] D. Boneh and J. Horwitz. *Generating a product of three primes with an unknown factorization*. In J. P. Buhler (ed.), Algorithmic Number Theory,

LNCS, pages 237–251, Berlin, Heidelberg, 1998. Springer Berlin Heidelberg. DOI:10.1007/BFb0054866.

[Bla79] G. R. Blakley. *Safeguarding cryptographic keys.* In Proc. International Workshop on Managing Requirements Knowledge, vol. 48 of AFIPS 1979, pages 313–317, 1979. DOI:10.1109/AFIPS.1979.98.

[BM99] M. Bellare and S. K. Miner. *A Forward-Secure Digital Signature Scheme.* In M. Wiener (ed.), Advances in Cryptology — CRYPTO' 99, vol. 1666 of LNCS, pages 431–448. Springer Berlin Heidelberg, 1999. DOI:10.1007/3-540-48405-1_28.

[BMW⁺18] J. v. Bulck, M. Minkin, O. Weisse, D. Genkin, B. Kasikci, F. Piessens, M. Silberstein, T. F. Wenisch, Y. Yarom, and R. Strackx. *Foreshadow: Extracting the Keys to the Intel SGX Kingdom with Transient Out-of-Order Execution.* In 27th USENIX Security Symposium (USENIX Security 18), page 991–1008, Baltimore, MD, 2018. USENIX Association.

[BN06] M. Bellare and G. Neven. *Multi-signatures in the Plain public-Key Model and a General Forking Lemma.* In Proc. 13th ACM Conference on Computer and Communications Security, CCS '06, pages 390–399. ACM, 2006. DOI:10.1145/1180405.1180453.

[BR07] M. Bellare and P. Rogaway. *Robust Computational Secret Sharing and a Unified Account of Classical Secret-sharing Goals.* In Proceedings of the 14th ACM Conference on Computer and Communications Security, CCS '07, pages 172–184, New York, NY, USA, 2007. ACM. DOI:10.1145/1315245.1315268.

[Bre12] E. Brewer. *CAP Twelve Years Later: How the "Rules" Have Changed.* Computer, 45:23–29, 01 2012. DOI:10.1109/MC.2012.37.

[CA78] L. Chen and A. Avizienis. *N-Version Programming: A Fault-Tolerance Approach to Reliability of Software Operation.* Digest FTCS-8: 8th Annual International Conference on Fault Tolerant Computing, pages 3–9, June 1978.

[Can01] R. Canetti. *Universally Composable Security: A New Paradigm for Cryptographic Protocols.* In Proc. 42nd IEEE Symposium on Foundations of Computer Science, FOCS '01, pages 136–145. IEEE Computer Society, 2001. DOI:10.1109/SFCS.2001.959888.

[CCD88] D. Chaum, C. Crépeau, and I. Damgard. *Multiparty Unconditionally Secure Protocols.* In Proceedings of the Twentieth Annual ACM Symposium on Theory of Computing, STOC '88, pages 11–19, New York, NY, USA, 1988. ACM. DOI:10.1145/62212.62214.

[CHH⁺17] C. Cremers, M. Horvat, J. Hoyland, S. Scott, and T. van der Merwe. *A Comprehensive Symbolic Analysis of TLS 1.3.* In Proceedings of the 2017 ACM SIGSAC Conference on Computer and Communications

Security, CCS '17, pages 1773–1788, New York, NY, USA, 2017. ACM. DOI:10.1145/3133956.3134063.

[CJRR99] S. Chari, C. S. Jutla, J. R. Rao, and P. Rohatgi. *Towards Sound Approaches to Counteract Power-Analysis Attacks*. In M. Wiener (ed.), Advances in Cryptology — CRYPTO' 99, vol. 1666 of LNCS, pages 398–412. Springer Berlin Heidelberg, 1999. DOI:10.1007/3-540-48405-1_26.

[CL02] M. Castro and B. Liskov. *Practical Byzantine Fault Tolerance and Proactive Recovery*. ACM Trans. Comput. Syst., 20(4):398–461, November 2002. DOI:10.1145/571637.571640.

[Com17] Common Criteria. *Common Criteria for Information Technology Security Evaluation*, April 2017. https://www.commoncriteriaportal.org/.

[CvH91] D. Chaum and E. van Heyst. *Group Signatures*. In D. W. Davies (ed.), Advances in Cryptology — EUROCRYPT '91, vol. 547 of LNCS, pages 257–265. Springer Berlin Heidelberg, 1991. DOI:10.1007/3-540-46416-6_22.

[DDF14] A. Duc, S. Dziembowski, and S. Faust. *Unifying Leakage Models: From Probing Attacks to Noisy Leakage*. In Advances in Cryptology — EUROCRYPT 2014, vol. 8441 of LNCS, pages 423–440. Springer Berlin Heidelberg, 2014. DOI:10.1007/978-3-642-55220-5_24.

[DDN03] D. Dolev, C. Dwork, and M. Naor. *Nonmalleable Cryptography*. SIAM Review, 45(4):727–784, 2003. DOI:10.1137/S0036144503429856.

[DDS87] D. Dolev, C. Dwork, and L. Stockmeyer. *On the Minimal Synchronism Needed for Distributed Consensus*. J. ACM, 34(1):77–97, January 1987. DOI:10.1145/7531.7533.

[DF90] Y. Desmedt and Y. Frankel. *Threshold cryptosystems*. In G. Brassard (ed.), Advances in Cryptology — CRYPTO' 89 Proceedings, vol. 435 of LNCS, pages 307–315. Springer New York, 1990. DOI:10.1007/0-387-34805-0_28.

[DJ97] Y. Desmedt and S. Jajodia. *Redistributing Secret Shares to New Access Structures and Its Applications*. Technical Report ISSE-TR-97-01, George Mason University, July 1997.

[DLFK+17] A. Delignat-Lavaud, C. Fournet, M. Kohlweiss, J. Protzenko, A. Rastogi, N. Swamy, S. Zanella-Béguelin, K. Bhargavan, J. Pan, and J. K. Zinzindohoué. *Implementing and proving the TLS 1.3 record layer*. In 2017 IEEE Symposium on Security and Privacy (SP), pages 463–482. IEEE, May 2017. DOI:10.1109/SP.2017.58.

[DLK+14] Z. Durumeric, F. Li, J. Kasten, J. Amann, J. Beekman, M. Payer, N. Weaver, D. Adrian, V. Paxson, M. Bailey, and J. A. Halderman. *The Matter of Heartbleed*. In Proc. 2014 Conference on Internet Measurement Conference, IMC '14, pages 475–488, New York, NY, USA, 2014. ACM. DOI:10.1145/2663716.2663755.

[Dou02] J. R. Douceur. *The Sybil Attack.* In P. Druschel, F. Kaashoek, and A. Rowstron (eds.), Peer-to-Peer Systems, pages 251–260. Springer Berlin Heidelberg, 2002. DOI:10.1007/3-540-45748-8_24.

[DSDFY94] A. De Santis, Y. Desmedt, Y. Frankel, and M. Yung. *How to Share a Function Securely.* In Proc. 26th Annual ACM Symposium on Theory of Computing, STOC '94, pages 522–533. ACM, 1994. DOI:10.1145/195058.195405.

[Fel87] P. Feldman. *A Practical Scheme for Non-interactive Verifiable Secret Sharing.* In Proc. 28th Annual Symposium on Foundations of Computer Science, SFCS '87, pages 427–438. IEEE Computer Society, 1987. DOI:10.1109/SFCS.1987.4.

[FHHW03] M. Fitzi, M. Hirt, T. Holenstein, and J. Wullschleger. *Two-Threshold Broadcast and Detectable Multi-party Computation.* In E. Biham (ed.), Advances in Cryptology — EUROCRYPT 2003, vol. 2656 of LNCS, pages 51–67, Berlin, Heidelberg, 2003. Springer Berlin Heidelberg. DOI:10.1007/3-540-39200-9_4.

[FLP85] M. J. Fischer, N. A. Lynch, and M. S. Paterson. *Impossibility of Distributed Consensus with One Faulty Process.* J. ACM, 32(2):374–382, April 1985. DOI:10.1145/3149.214121.

[FNP04] M. J. Freedman, K. Nissim, and B. Pinkas. *Efficient private matching and set intersection.* In International conference on the theory and applications of cryptographic techniques, pages 1–19. Springer, 2004.

[Fra90] Y. Frankel. *A Practical Protocol for Large Group Oriented Networks.* In J.-J. Quisquater and J. Vandewalle (eds.), Advances in Cryptology — EUROCRYPT '89, LNCS, pages 56–61, Berlin, Heidelberg, 1990. Springer Berlin Heidelberg. DOI:10.1007/3-540-46885-4_8.

[GJKR99] R. Gennaro, S. Jarecki, H. Krawczyk, and T. Rabin. *Secure Distributed Key Generation for Discrete-Log Based Cryptosystems.* In J. Stern (ed.), Advances in Cryptology — EUROCRYPT '99, vol. 1592 of LNCS, pages 295–310, Berlin, Heidelberg, 1999. Springer Berlin Heidelberg. DOI:10.1007/3-540-48910-X_21.

[GMR85] S. Goldwasser, S. Micali, and C. Rackoff. *The Knowledge Complexity of Interactive Proof-systems.* In Proc. 17th Annual ACM Symposium on Theory of Computing, STOC '85, pages 291–304. ACM, 1985. DOI:10.1145/22145.22178.

[GMW87] O. Goldreich, S. Micali, and A. Wigderson. *How to Play ANY Mental Game or A Completeness Theorem for Protocols with Honest Majority.* In Proc. 19th Annual ACM Symposium on Theory of Computing, STOC '87, pages

218–229. ACM, 1987. DOI:10.1145/28395.28420.

[GRJK00] R. Gennaro, T. Rabin, S. Jarecki, and H. Krawczyk. *Robust and Efficient Sharing of RSA Functions.* Journal of Cryptology, 13(2):273–300, Mar 2000. DOI:10.1007/s001459910011.

[Gro16] C. T. Group. *NIST Cryptographic Standards and Guidelines Development Process.* NISTIR 7977, March 2016. DOI:10.6028/NIST.IR.7977.

[Gue09] S. Gueron. *Intel's New AES Instructions for Enhanced Performance and Security.* In O. Dunkelman (ed.), Fast Software Encryption, 16th International Workshop, FSE 2009, vol. 5665 of LNCS, pages 51–66. Springer, 2009. DOI:10.1007/978-3-642-03317-9_4.

[HJKY95] A. Herzberg, S. Jarecki, H. Krawczyk, and M. Yung. *Proactive Secret Sharing Or: How to Cope With Perpetual Leakage.* In D. Coppersmith (ed.), Advances in Cryptology — CRYPT0' 95, pages 339–352. Springer Berlin Heidelberg, 1995. DOI:10.1007/3-540-44750-4_27.

[HM00] M. Hirt and U. Maurer. *Player Simulation and General Adversary Structures in Perfect Multiparty Computation.* Journal of Cryptology, 13(1):31–60, Jan 2000. DOI:10.1007/s001459910003.

[HSH$^+$09] J. A. Halderman, S. D. Schoen, N. Heninger, W. Clarkson, W. Paul, J. A. Calandrino, A. J. Feldman, J. Appelbaum, and E. W. Felten. *Lest We Remember: Cold-boot Attacks on Encryption Keys.* Commun. ACM, 52(5):91–98, May 2009. DOI:10.1145/1506409.1506429.

[IN83] K. Itakura and K. Nakamura. *A public-key cryptosystem suitable for digital multisignatures.* In NEC J. Res. Dev. 71, pages 1–8, Oct. 1983.

[Int18] Intel Corporation. *Software Guard Extention (SGX).* https://software.intel.com/en-us/sgx, 2018.

[ISN89] M. Ito, A. Saito, and T. Nishizeki. *Secret sharing scheme realizing general access structure.* Electronics and Communications in Japan (Part III: Fundamental Electronic Science), 72(9):56–64, 1989. DOI:10.1002/ecjc.4430720906.

[ISO12] ISO. *ISO/IEC 19790:2012, Information technology – Security techniques – Security requirements for cryptographic modules.* https://www.iso.org/standard/52906.html, August 2012.

[ISO16] ISO. *ISO/IEC 19592-1:2016, Information technology – Security techniques – Secret sharing – Part 1: General.* https://www.iso.org/standard/65422.html, 2016.

[ISO17] ISO. *ISO/IEC 19592-2:2017, Information technology – Security techniques – Secret sharing – Part 2: Fundamental mechanisms.* https://www.iso.org/standard/65425.html, 2017.

[ISW03] Y. Ishai, A. Sahai, and D. A. Wagner. *Private Circuits: Securing Hardware against Probing Attacks*. In Advances in Cryptology — CRYPTO 2003, vol. 2729 of LNCS, pages 463–481. Springer Berlin Heidelberg, 2003. DOI:10.1007/978-3-540-45146-4_27.

[JB99] A. Juels and J. Brainard. *Client puzzles: A Cryptographic countermeasure against connection depletion attacks*. In Network and distributed system security symposium — NDSS'99, vol. 99, pages 151–168. Internet Society, 1999.

[KF95] N. Kolettis and N. D. Fulton. *Software Rejuvenation: Analysis, Module and Applications*. In Proc. 25th International Symposium on Fault-Tolerant Computing, FTCS '95, pages 381–390. IEEE, 1995. DOI:10.1109/FTCS.1995.466961.

[KGG⁺18] P. Kocher, D. Genkin, D. Gruss, W. Haas, M. Hamburg, M. Lipp, S. Mangard, T. Prescher, M. Schwarz, and Y. Yarom. *Spectre Attacks: Exploiting Speculative Execution*. ArXiv e-prints, January 2018.

[Kis13] R. Kissel. *Glossary of Key Information Security Terms*. NISTIR 7298 Revision 2, May 2013. DOI:10.6028/NIST.IR.7298r2.

[KK07] I. Koren and C. M. Krishna. *Fault-Tolerant Systems*. Morgan Kaufmann Publishers Inc., 1st edition, 2007.

[Koc96] P. C. Kocher. *Timing Attacks on Implementations of Diffie-Hellman, RSA, DSS, and Other Systems*. In N. Koblitz (ed.), Advances in Cryptology — CRYPTO '96, vol. 1109 of LNCS, pages 104–113. Springer Berlin Heidelberg, 1996. DOI:10.1007/3-540-68697-5_9.

[KPVV16] T. Kaufmann, H. Pelletier, S. Vaudenay, and K. Villegas. *When Constant-Time Source Yields Variable-Time Binary: Exploiting Curve25519-donna Built with MSVC 2015*. In Cryptology and Network Security — CANS 2016, vol. 10052 of LNCS, pages 573–582. Springer Berlin Heidelberg, 2016. DOI:10.1007/978-3-319-48965-0_36.

[Kra94] H. Krawczyk. *Secret Sharing Made Short*. In D. R. Stinson (ed.), Advances in Cryptology — CRYPTO '93, vol. 573 of LNCS, pages 136–146. Springer Berlin Heidelberg, 1994. DOI:10.1007/3-540-48329-2_12.

[Lam06] L. Lamport. *Lower bounds for asynchronous consensus*. Distributed Computing, 19(2):104–125, Oct 2006. DOI:10.1007/s00446-006-0155-x.

[LS04] B. Littlewood and L. Strigini. *Redundancy and Diversity in Security*. In P. Samarati, P. Ryan, D. Gollmann, and R. Molva (eds.), Computer Security – ESORICS 2004, pages 423–438. Springer Berlin Heidelberg, 2004. DOI:10.1007/978-3-540-30108-0_26.

[LSG⁺18] M. Lipp, M. Schwarz, D. Gruss, T. Prescher, W. Haas, S. Mangard, P. Kocher, D. Genkin, Y. Yarom, and M. Hamburg. *Meltdown*. ArXiv e-prints, January

2018.

[LSP82] L. Lamport, R. Shostak, and M. Pease. *The Byzantine Generals Problem.* ACM Transactions on Programming Languages and Systems, 4(3):382–401, July 1982. DOI:10.1145/357172.357176.

[Lyn89] N. Lynch. *A Hundred Impossibility Proofs for Distributed Computing.* In Proc. 8th Annual ACM Symposium on Principles of Distributed Computing, PODC '89, pages 1–28. ACM, 1989. DOI:10.1145/72981.72982.

[MBTM17] K. A. McKay, L. Bassham, M. S. Turan, and N. Mouha. *NISTIR 8114 — Report on Lightweight Cryptography*, 2017. DOI:10.6028/NIST.IR.8114.

[MOR01] S. Micali, K. Ohta, and L. Reyzin. *Accountable-subgroup Multisignatures: Extended Abstract.* In Proc. 8th ACM Conference on Computer and Communications Security, CCS '01, pages 245–254. ACM, 2001. DOI:10.1145/501983.502017.

[Mor11] T. Morris. *Trusted Platform Module.* In H. C. A. van Tilborg and S. Jajodia (eds.), Encyclopedia of Cryptography and Security, 2nd Ed., pages 1332–1335. Springer, 2011. DOI:10.1007/978-1-4419-5906-5_796.

[NIS01] NIST. *Security Requirements for Cryptographic Modules, Federal Information Processing Standard (FIPS) 140-2*, 2001. DOI:10.6028/NIST.FIPS.140-2.

[NIS17] NIST. *Post-quantum Cryptography Project.* https://csrc.nist.gov/projects/post-quantum-cryptography, 2017.

[NIS18a] NIST. *Automated Cryptographic Validation Protocol.* https://github.com/usnistgov/ACVP, 2018.

[NIS18b] NIST. *Automated Cryptographic Validation Testing.* https://csrc.nist.gov/projects/acvt/, 2018.

[NIS18c] NIST. *Cryptographic Module Validation Program.* https://csrc.nist.gov/projects/cryptographic-module-validation-program, 2018.

[NRR06] S. Nikova, C. Rechberger, and V. Rijmen. *Threshold Implementations Against Side-Channel Attacks and Glitches.* In P. Ning, S. Qing, and N. Li (eds.), Information and Communications Security — ICICS 2006, vol. 4307 of LNCS, pages 529–545. Springer Berlin Heidelberg, 2006. DOI:10.1007/11935308_38.

[NVD14] NVD. *National Vulnerability Database — CVE-2014-0160.* https://nvd.nist.gov/vuln/detail/CVE-2014-0160, 2014.

[NVD18a] NVD. *National Vulnerability Database — CVE-2017-5715.* https://nvd.nist.gov/vuln/detail/CVE-2017-5715, 2018.

[NVD18b] NVD. *National Vulnerability Database — CVE-2017-5753.*

https://nvd.nist.gov/vuln/detail/CVE-2017-5753, 2018.

[NVD18c] NVD.   *National   Vulnerability   Database   —   CVE-2017-5754.*
          https://nvd.nist.gov/vuln/detail/CVE-2017-5754, 2018.

[OY91]   R. Ostrovsky and M. Yung. *How to Withstand Mobile Virus Attacks
          (Extended Abstract).* In Proc. 10th Annual ACM Symposium on Prin-
          ciples of Distributed Computing, PODC '91, pages 51–59. ACM, 1991.
          DOI:10.1145/112600.112605.

[Ped91]   T. P. Pedersen. *A Threshold Cryptosystem without a Trusted Party.* In
          D. W. Davies (ed.), Advances in Cryptology — EUROCRYPT '91,
          vol. 547 of LNCS, pages 522–526. Springer Berlin Heidelberg, 1991.
          DOI:10.1007/3-540-46416-6_47.

[Ped92]   T. P. Pedersen. *Non-Interactive and Information-Theoretic Secure Verifiable
          Secret Sharing.* In J. Feigenbaum (ed.), Advances in Cryptology — CRYPTO
          '91, vol. 576 of LNCS, pages 129–140. Springer Berlin Heidelberg, 1992.
          DOI:10.1007/3-540-46766-1_9.

[Por18]   T. Pornin. *BearSSL — Constant-Time Mul.* https://bearssl.org/ctmul.html,
          2018.

[PSL80]   M. Pease, R. Shostak, and L. Lamport. *Reaching Agreement in the Presence
          of Faults.* J. ACM, 27(2):228–234, April 1980. DOI:10.1145/322186.322188.

[PW92]   B. Pfitzmann and M. Waidner. *Unconditional Byzantine agreement for any
          number of faulty processors.* In A. Finkel and M. Jantzen (eds.), STACS 92,
          pages 337–350. Springer Berlin Heidelberg, 1992. DOI:10.1007/3-540-55210-
          3_195.

[Rab83]   M. O. Rabin. *Randomized Byzantine Generals.* In Proc. 24th Annual
          Symposium on Foundations of Computer Science, SFCS '83, pages 403–409.
          IEEE Computer Society, 1983. DOI:10.1109/SFCS.1983.48.

[Rad97]   J. Radatz. *The IEEE Standard Dictionary of Electrical and Electronics Terms.*
          IEEE Standards Office, 6th edition, 1997.

[RSA78]   R. L. Rivest, A. Shamir, and L. Adleman. *A method for obtaining digital
          signatures and public-key cryptosystems.* Communications of the ACM,
          21(2):120–126, 1978. DOI:10.1145/359340.359342.

[RSWO17] E. Ronen., A. Shamir, A.-O. Weingarten, and C. O'Flynn. *IoT Goes Nuclear:
          Creating a ZigBee Chain Reaction.* IEEE Symposium on Security and Privacy,
          pages 195–212, 2017. DOI:10.1109/SP.2017.14.

[SA09]   N. R. Sunitha and B. B. Amberker.   *Forward-Secure Multi-signatures.*
          In M. Parashar and S. K. Aggarwal (eds.), Distributed Computing and
          Internet Technology, pages 89–99. Springer Berlin Heidelberg, 2009.

DOI:10.1007/978-3-540-89737-8_9.

[Sau34] R. Saunders. *Poor Richard's Almanack — 1735*. Benjamin Franklin, 1734.

[Sch90] C. P. Schnorr. *Efficient Identification and Signatures for Smart Cards*. In G. Brassard (ed.), Advances in Cryptology — CRYPTO'89 Proceedings, vol. 435 of LNCS, pages 239–252. Springer New York, 1990. DOI:10.1007/0-387-34805-0_22.

[Sch99] B. Schoenmakers. *A Simple Publicly Verifiable Secret Sharing Scheme and Its Application to Electronic Voting*. In M. Wiener (ed.), Advances in Cryptology — CRYPTO '99, vol. 1666 of LNCS, pages 148–164. Springer Berlin Heidelberg, 1999. DOI:10.1007/3-540-48405-1_10.

[Sha97] W. Shakespeare. *An excellent conceited Tragedie of Romeo and Juliet*. Printed by John Danter, London, 1597.

[Sha79] A. Shamir. *How to Share a Secret*. Communications of the ACM, 22(11):612–613, Nov 1979. DOI:10.1145/359168.359176.

[Sho00] V. Shoup. *Practical Threshold Signatures*. In B. Preneel (ed.), Advances in Cryptology — EUROCRYPT 2000, vol. 1807 of LNCS, pages 207–220. Springer Berlin Heidelberg, 2000. DOI:10.1007/3-540-45539-6_15.

[SNV07] P. Sousa, N. F. Neves, and P. Verissimo. *Hidden Problems of Asynchronous Proactive Recovery*. Proc. 3rd Workshop on on Hot Topics in System Dependability, 2007.

[Sta96] M. Stadler. *Publicly Verifiable Secret Sharing*. In U. Maurer (ed.), Advances in Cryptology — EUROCRYPT '96, vol. 1070 of LNCS, pages 190–199. Springer Berlin Heidelberg, 1996. DOI:10.1007/3-540-68339-9_17.

[SZ05] F. B. Schneider and L. Zhou. *Implementing Trustworthy Services Using Replicated State Machines*. IEEE Security and Privacy, 3(5):34–43, September 2005. DOI:10.1109/MSP.2005.125.

[tC96] U. S. 104th Congress. *Information Technology Management Reform Act. Public Law 104–106, Section 5131*, 1996. https://www.dol.gov/ocfo/media/regs/ITMRA.pdf.

[TJ11] H. C. A. Tilborg and S. Jajodia. *Encyclopedia of Cryptography and Security*. Springer Publishing Company, Incorporated, 2nd edition, 2011. DOI:10.1007/978-1-4419-5906-5.

[Vas15] A. Vassilev. *Cryptographic Validation Challenges With Brittle Algorithms*. https://csrc.nist.gov/groups/ST/lwc-workshop2015/presentations/session5-vassilev.pdf, July 2015.

[VCB$^+$13] G. S. Veronese, M. Correia, A. N. Bessani, L. C. Lung, and P. Veríssimo.

Efficient Byzantine Fault-Tolerance. IEEE Transactions on Computers, 62(1):16–30, 01 2013. DOI:10.1109/TC.2011.221.

[vdGP88] J. van de Graaf and R. Peralta. *A Simple and Secure Way to Show the Validity of Your Public Key.* In C. Pomerance (ed.), Advances in Cryptology — CRYPTO '87, vol. 293 of LNCS, pages 128–134. Springer Berlin Heidelberg, 1988. DOI:10.1007/3-540-48184-2_9.

[Ver18] Verizon. *2018 Data Breach Investigations Report.* https://www.verizonenterprise.com/verizon-insights-lab/dbir/, 2018.

[VMB18] A. Vassilev, N. Mouha, and L. Brandão. *Psst, Can You Keep a Secret?* IEEE Computer, 51(1):94–97, January 2018. DOI:10.1109/MC.2018.1151029.

[Yao82] A. C. Yao. *Protocols for secure computations.* In 23rd Annual Symposium on Foundations of Computer Science, SFCS '82, pages 160–164, 11 1982. DOI:10.1109/SFCS.1982.88.

[Yao86] A. C. Yao. *How to Generate and Exchange Secrets.* In Proc. 27th Annual Symposium on Foundations of Computer Science, SFCS '86, pages 162–167. IEEE Computer Society, 1986. DOI:10.1109/SFCS.1986.25.